AR 3 0 2001

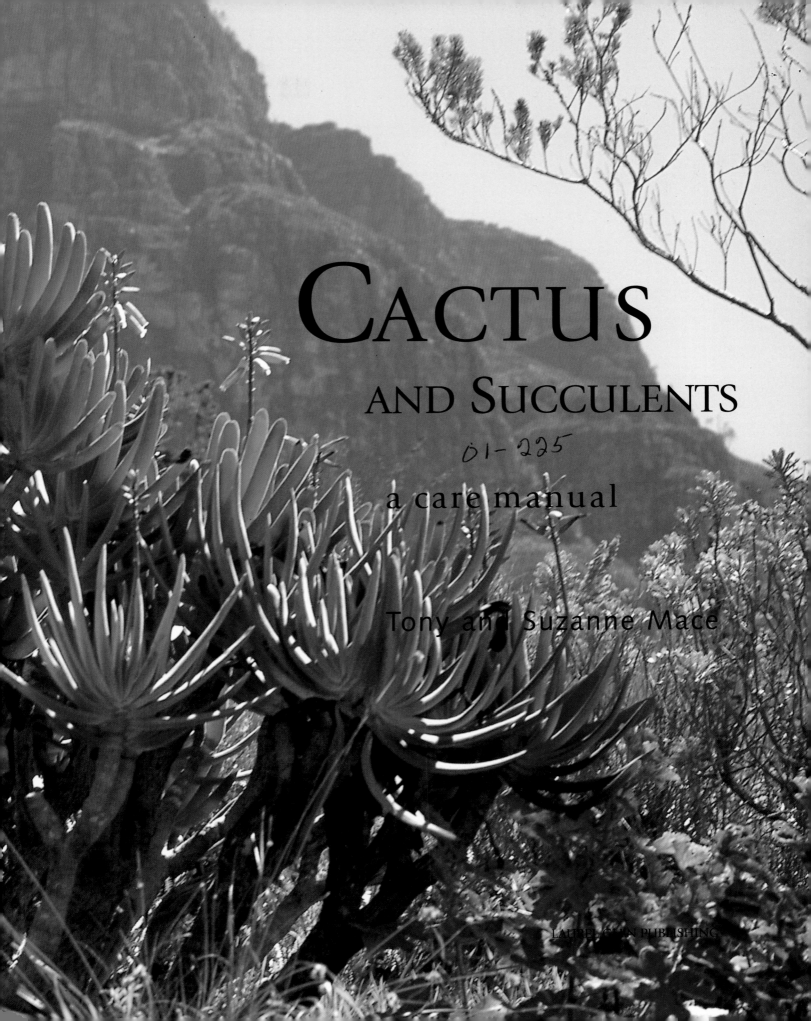

CACTUS
AND SUCCULENTS

01-225

a care manual

Tony and Suzanne Mace

LAUREL GLEN PUBLISHING

First published in
the United States, 1998
by Laurel Glen Publishing
5880 Oberlin Drive, Suite 400
San Diego, CA 92121-9653
1-800-284-3580

First published in
Great Britain in 1998
by Hamlyn
an imprint of Reed Consumer Books Limited
Michelin House, 81 Fulham Road,
London SW3 6RB
and Auckland, Melbourne,
Singapore and Toronto

Produced by Toppan
Printed in China

Publishing Director
Laura Bamford
Executive Editor
Julian Brown
Assistant Editor
Karen O'Grady
Executive Art Editor
Mark Winwood
Art Director
Keith Martin
Production Controller
Julie Hadingham
Picture Research
Liz Fowler
Design
Ruth Hope
Special photography
Peter Myers
and Sean Myers

Library of Congress
Cataloging-in-Publication Data

Mace, Tony.
Cactus and succulents :
a care manual / Tony and Suzanne Mace.
p.   cm.
Includes bibliographical
references and index.
ISBN 1-57145-619-8
1. Cactus--Handbooks, manuals, etc.
2. Succulents plants--Handbooks,
manuals, etc.
I. Mace, Suzanne. II. Title.
SB438.M235   1998
635.9'3356--dc 21   98-18395
CIP

Contents

Introduction

Suzanne Mace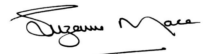

Dr. Tony Mace

The exotic nature of these unusual plants includes their vivid, often extraordinary, flowers—one of their most coveted features.

Then there is the appeal of the strangely beautiful forms, from the numerous gem-like beauties to the intriguingly grotesque. The many bizarre shapes range from a claret cup to a barrel, a sea urchin to a shark's jaw; a donkey's ear to a bird; some look for all the world like "flowering stones," a perfect camouflage in their native habitat.

The convolutions, bearded woolliness, and even the threat of strange and fierce spines bring a dimension not seen in other plants. Adding to their fascination, cacti and succulents originate in exotic parts of

Opposite: *Morangaya pensilis* is an unusual endemic cactus from the tip of the Baja peninsula in California.

the world. They are notable for using their clever adaptations to withstand extreme temperatures in some of the most remote and arid places on earth.

The novelty of these features has always attracted enthusiasts to collecting cacti and succulents. Equally important, many of these plants are easy to care for and have a forgiving nature. Others present a great, but not impossible, challenge to the more experienced collector.

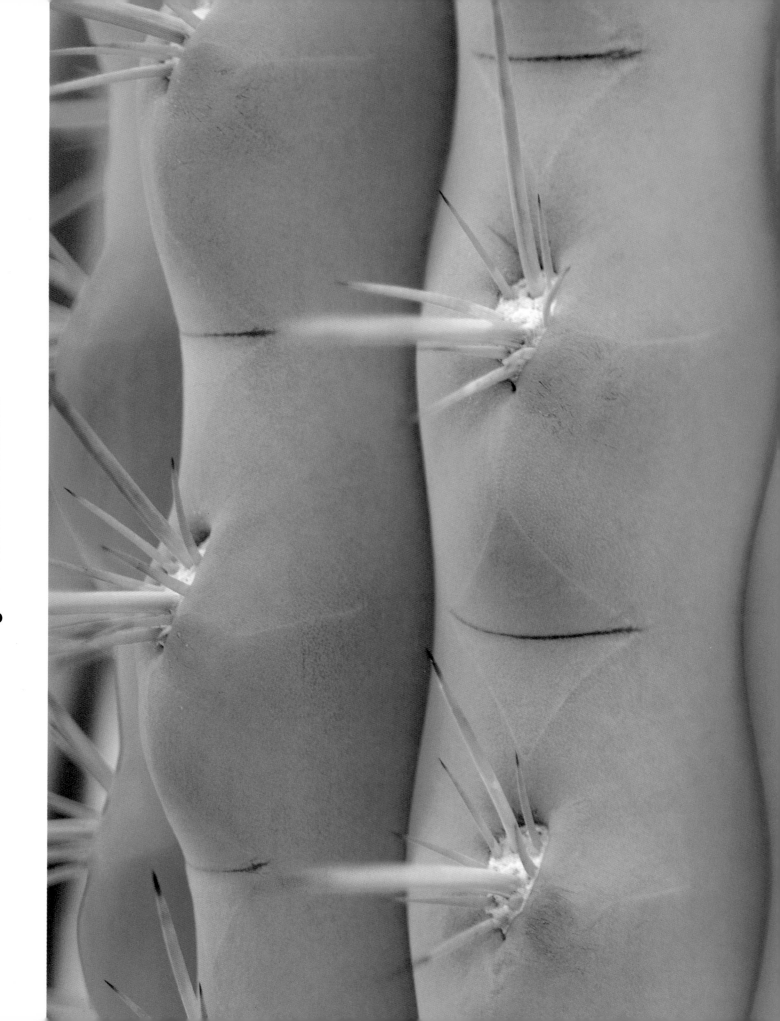

What are Cacti and Succulents?

What Are Cacti and Succulents?

Succulent plants, of which cacti are but one family, have developed ways of storing water so that, in a period of temporary water shortage, they are able to draw on their reserves, unlike many ordinary plants that will quickly wilt and die without water.

Their often strange appearance is a result of the modifications they have evolved to enable them to store water: thickened stems, leaves, or roots. Various other modifications either facilitate this storage of water or, equally importantly, reduce its loss. Cells of succulent plants are able to survive a greater variation of their water content than are the cells of ordinary plants. They frequently have a thickened epidermis, or one covered in hairs or a waxy coating that reduces water loss. The dense covering of spines has its role in reducing the effect of intense solar heat on the plants by providing a partial shading effect.

Biochemical differences

One modification in succulent plants occurs at a less obvious biochemical level, which operates in a way that is very different from the chemistry of most plants.

Plants produce food by photosynthesis, combining carbon dioxide and water to produce sugars and starches, releasing oxygen in the process. The water is absorbed largely through the roots, while the carbon dioxide is taken in through minute apertures, called stomata, in the leaves. This occurs during daylight when the energy of sunlight drives the process. At the same time a lot of water evaporates through the leaves; this does not matter for ordinary plants because there is plenty of water available to replace the loss.

In the case of succulent plants, many have developed a modified process that enables them to keep their stomata closed during the day, and to open them only at night. The photosynthetic process in these plants is called Crassulacean Acid Metabolism (CAM). Here, carbon dioxide is absorbed at night rather than during the day, and is also combined into various organic acids. During the day this acid is turned into sugars by the action of photosynthesis. Interestingly, this phenomenon was known to ancient apothecaries: they realized that the taste of succulent plants varied greatly with the time of day they were collected, and this was due to the changing acid content.

This modified photosynthetic process has one very important effect for cultivators of succulents: it works best when there is a considerable difference between daytime and nighttime temperatures; hence succulents thrive where there are certain extremes of temperature. This explains why many growers in tropical countries with high nighttime

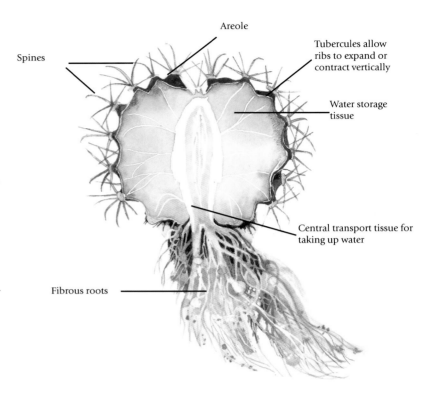

Spines
Areole
Tubercules allow ribs to expand or contract vertically
Water storage tissue
Central transport tissue for taking up water
Fibrous roots

Cross section of a cactus showing the internal structure.

temperatures find some succulents quite difficult to grow, when conditions otherwise appear to be ideal.

Where are cacti and succulents found?

Cacti: The Cactaceae are strictly a New World family. Their native habitats are found all the way from southern Canada down to Patagonia, but their peak distribution is in Mexico and some of the South American Andean countries. Cacti have been introduced into many other dry areas of the world where some have multiplied very rapidly and become seriously invasive, in Australia, for example.

Succulents: As for succulent plants, they are found in many areas of the world,

but the largest concentrations are in Mexico and South America, particularly the Andean countries. Significant numbers occur in many South and Central American countries, as well as in East Africa, Arabia, Madagascar, and India. Many small islands, such as the Canary Islands, also have a unique indigenous succulent flora.

Interestingly, the deserts of Australia have few succulents (other than cacti), possibly because the period between rains is too long and unreliable. The flora there mainly comprises very rapidly growing annual plants with long-term viability seeds—an alternative survival strategy for such conditions.

Succulent Plant Families

Succulence occurs in many families of plants. One of the most familiar is the cactus family (Cactaceae). It is not strictly correct to use the term "cacti and succulents," as cacti are already included in the term succulent. Virtually all cacti are succulent, although just a few of the very primitive ones have large, not very succulent leaves and can photosynthesize by the normal (non-CAM) route. The Cactaceae are distinguished botanically from other plant families primarily by their flower and seed structure.

The easiest way to identify whether a plant is a cactus is to look for a structure called the areole. This is a growth point on the cactus from which new offsets, flowers, and spines arise. It varies considerably in size from species to species, but frequently displays at least a small amount of wool or small hairs. (Some other succulent plants, such as euphorbias, also grow spines but do not have the areole structure of a cactus.)

Other families of plants have significant numbers of succulent species, but may also have non-succulent ones. Typical examples of this are the Euphorbiaceae or Asphodelaceae. The total number of species of succulents is very large: at least 2,000 species of cacti and 20,000 species of succulents occur in other plant families. Only a small fraction of these plants are in this book, but some are included from the following families: Agavaceae, Aizoaceae (Mesembryanthemaceae), Apocynaceae, Asclepiadiaceae, Asphodelaceae, Asteraceae, Cactaceae, Crassulaceae, Dracenaceae, and Euphorbiaceae.

We should point out that certain groups of plants could be included here with these plants but are traditionally not regarded as succulents, in itself an imprecise term that is open to interpretation. One is the bromeliads, many of which exhibit at least some degree of succulence and frequently occur in similar habitats. Another is the orchids, which store water as well as food in their pseudobulbs and are often able to survive periods of drought. Many species of bulbous plants grow alongside succulents in semi-desert areas, but widening the scope to include these plants is beyond the purpose of this book.

A variety of growth forms and types of succulents.

Contorted

Cespitose

Crassula

Conophytum

Columnar

Pendent

Arborescent

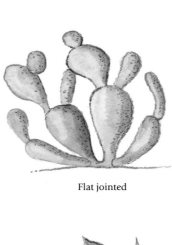

Flat jointed

Globose cespitose

Arching

Mesophyte

Globose

Cylindric

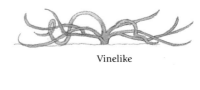

Vinelike

Creeping

Diffuse

Decumbent

Bushy

Candelabra

Echeveria

Haworthia

Growth Forms

CRISTATE PLANT

This phenomenon occurs when the growing point of a plant repeatedly divides, forming a continuous line of growth rather than the more normal single point. Such "witches brooms" are known in a number of plant families, but are a common occurrence among cacti and some other groups of succulent plants.

As the fan of growth expands it forms a convoluted mass. Some collectors specialize in these forms and seek out rare new forms. There is a tendency for the ends of the fan to be pushed down into the soil, making the plant vulnerable to rot, so it is not uncommon for them to be grafted onto a taller cactus in order to keep the growing point away from the damp soil.

What causes this growth form to occur in the first place is not certain. It is probably not an inherited characteristic and such plants are usually propagated by vegetative means either by cuttings or by grafting. Cristate plants are usually somewhat reluctant to flower. Very occasionally cristate flowers can be developed as well.

Opposite: More growth forms and types of succulent.

Right: *Aloe plicatilis*, an unusual aloe from South Africa; it will eventually form a small bush.

Below: *Opuntia chlorotica* in its natural habitat—the Sonoran Desert.

MONSTROSE PLANTS

These plants are somewhat related to the cristate plants, but in this case the growth points separate before dividing again. This results in plants with very many growth points. This occurs mostly in a few species of *Cereus*. Another variant on this theme occurs on some species of *Opuntia* where every areole produces a shoot resulting in masses of tiny offsets. Still other rib-and-spine derangements occur in plants such as the monstrose form of *Lophocereus schottii*, which is almost completely spineless.

Why Grow Cacti and Succulents?

There is a fascination in watching any plant grow, as it matures into a well-grown specimen and an object of beauty. When it comes to growing cacti and succulents there is a particular appeal on several levels.

Find a daily source of wonder

Their exotic nature, often unusual colors and forms, and very beautiful flowers can be a constant source of wonderment and enjoyment.

Your curiosity is stimulated, then your questions are answered as a plant grows and changes in your care, and you begin to understand how and why it responds in a certain way, the way that is natural for it.

Meet the challenge

The requirements of growing these exotic plants set them apart. Their cultivation in less than favorable climates presents some challenges to be overcome.

However, it is quite possible to grow them successfully, and you can to your great personal satisfaction.

Enjoy the anticipation

Slow-growing cacti and succulents may take many years to become fully mature plants. This characteristic is shared by only a relatively few groups of plants: bonsai trees and some alpines come to mind.

For those with patience, little can compare with the excitement felt when for the first time a cactus plant, which you may have looked after for thirty years, finally produces a magnificent flower.

Above: *Dudleya pachyphytum,* a choice *Dudleya* from an island off the coast of California.

Left: *Mammillaria multidigita*—a species that is prone to clumping.

Grow plants well suited to modern living

Practical considerations make cacti and succulents especially suitable plants for cultivation in modern homes. You can leave cacti and succulents for a few weeks while you go on vacation without making arrangements for them to be watered. On your return, they will not be wilting or dead, like most other plants.

Also, space may be limited in today's homes, and it is quite possible to grow a very large number of cacti and succulent species in a small space. All that is needed is careful selection of miniature species and forms. There are many from which to choose.

Focus on one aspect

Like people with other multifaceted interests, cacti and succulent enthusiasts derive pleasure from focusing on specific aspects of the subject. Some people become interested in seed raising and propagation; others specialize in a particular group of plants; while still others become avid exhibitors, endeavoring to grow the finest specimens in order to win trophies.

"New eyes" through travel

For those who travel, it is fascinating and educational to visit areas where cacti and succulents grow naturally. A new depth of understanding is to be gained from seeing the plants in their native habitats. It may even be possible to search for rare species in habitat. Remember, most countries have severe restrictions on removing plants and plant material from the wild to help conserve the plants in their habitats. Of course, there are no restrictions on photographing these plants in their spectacular natural settings. Organized field trips are available in North America and South Africa.

People all over the world are interested in these plants and they are usually only too happy to meet, or communicate with, other lovers of cacti and succulents to discuss their favorite plants. This is a source of contacts and friends worldwide.

Join a local group

On a local level, groups meet regularly to discuss the various aspects of collecting cacti and succulents. Here is a valuable and close-to-home source of information and help for you.

Among the activities, guest speakers may be invited to entertain and educate. Local mini-shows are also sometimes arranged.

Outings and open days enable the group to visit cactus nurseries, or even other growers' collections to see how their plants are doing. Joining in with all these activities gives you good feedback, which you can relate to your own plants regarding their appearance or unusual behavior.

Tree aloes used as horticultural subjects in South Africa.

In the group, you can easily, often cheaply, increase your collection. Collectors bring reasonably priced plants and other items for sale at these meetings.

Many of the plants are so long lived that they are often passed on from collector to collector. The original owner may have stopped keeping plants through old age, or the plant may have become too big to manage. But what do you do with a plant that is too big? You will derive your own pleasure from growing and caring for these strangely beautiful living things. Cacti and succulents have a special place in the affections of thousands of collectors, and this book will give you practical advice and guidance so you, too, can achieve success with these plants.

Myths and Urban Legends

The Aztecs and the Incas

Not all myths about cacti are modern. Some are very ancient indeed. The cactus was an important symbol to both the Aztecs in Mexico and to the Incas in Peru, and its image of healing and divination can still be seen on many of their buildings, pottery, and other artifacts. In the *Codex Magliabecchi*, which dates from just after the Conquest, Mayahuel, the Aztec goddess of pulque (the poor-man's intoxicating drink, similar to tequila; both made from the maguey cactus or agave), is shown seated on a shell with a serpent and a tortoise; behind them rises a flowering plant.

Another feature of some cacti was even more important. Some contain hallucinogenic alkaloids, drugs that came to be used in religious ceremonies. The small tuberous peyote cactus, *Lophorphora williamsii*, from which mescaline is extracted, could heighten perception, and so quicken and intensify the process of reaching the deities. Since the priest caste knew how to manipulate these and other vision-inducing drugs they had great power.

Cacti thus had particular significance for these ancient civilizations, who elevated them to sacred and god-given plants. Indeed, some Native Americans still use certain cacti in this way. The Huichol Indians of west Mexico consider the peyote cactus to be divine and still make pilgrimages in search of it.

Above: The alkaloids in some cacti have hallucinogenic properties, which has resulted in them being used in religious ceremonies.

Opposite: Some American-Indian tribes living in Sonora depended on fruits of the *Carnegia gigantea* as an important food source.

Myths and Urban Legends?

Cacti have attracted false rumors and legends right up to the present time. Interestingly, some myths seem to stir deep-rooted fears, while others present cacti in a protective role. These myths often form the basis of questions we are asked repeatedly. We think it is important to dispel them:

"Cacti flower only once every seven years."
This is the most often heard statement, and it is total nonsense. It may have arisen due to a combination of several facts: some cacti do need to be quite large before they will flower; and cacti grown in poor light are reluctant to flower. Additionally, because of the very exotic nature of cacti and succulents and because, also exotic, orchids usually take a number of years to reach maturity and therefore flower, the two families seem to have been lumped together.

Cacti, like most plants, flower only when they reach maturity and will then flower once a year or in some cases several times a year. The length of time to reach maturity can be as little as two years for free-flowering *rebutias* or as much as forty years or so for some of the tree-like species.

For a minority of species it is very difficult to get the conditions right to persuade them to flower at all in cultivation. The most common reason is because the species is one that occurs naturally at very high altitudes where it is used to very high light intensities and extreme swings in day and night temperatures.

A slightly larger group of plants needs very good conditions in order to flower, conditions that may be met in some years but not in others. These plants are likely to flower occasionally in cultivation; some growers with favorably situated greenhouses are more likely to succeed than others.

A further possible source of this old wives' tale is probably connected with the monocarpic succulents, such as agaves. The rosette or head of leaves, which will eventually flower, may take anywhere between ten to forty years to reach maturity; then a massive terminal flower spike is produced, hence the name century plant, although it is improbable that any rosettes would actually be this old before flowering. The head of leaves dies after flowering.

"Cacti don't need water."
Cacti *do* need water, like any other living thing. The often repeated belief is that cacti don't need water, "because they come from the desert."

First, of course they need water; how else do they manage to live, and grow? Like humans, their tissue is made up predominantly of water.

Secondly, cacti come from arid regions of the earth, not deserts. In these arid areas there is often restricted rainfall or it comes only at certain times of the year. It is the nature of cacti that they can withstand not being watered for a long time—but not forever. It is also their nature that in times of plenty they can expand and store water for the times when it will be dry and they can then call on their reserves. The ribbing on a cactus is designed for this very event. It expands and contracts; in very good times it makes more ribs at the top of the plants. Note: Do not forget they can be overwatered.

"Cacti protect you from the radiation of computer screens."
This rather peculiar rumor is a fairly recent one. We are not quite sure in what way such a mechanism would work; perhaps the spines were supposed to collect ions?

We wonder if this myth has arisen from the use of plants to raise the humidity in very dry office environments which helps reduce the effect of irritating negative ionization of the atmosphere. If this is how the myth started, then cacti are perhaps the least likely plants to be effective in this way.

"A cactus exploded and released a horde of tarantulas."
This strange urban legend has repeatedly surfaced on the Internet. While spiders do build nests among cactus spines, we think somebody was playing a practical joke with this one.

Opposite: The eagle, the snake and the cactus all appear in Mexican state symbols.

Right: Early illustration of the genus *Opuntia*.

Below right: The fruits of *Opuntia*, also called prickly pear, are frequently eaten.

"Cactus spines are poisonous."
Cactus spines are *not* poisonous. This myth probably arose because some people have gotten an infection in the place where the spine punctured. Very rarely would someone contract septicemia; long before it reached that stage a doctor or hospital should have been consulted.

The role of cacti and succulents in myth and legend from the earliest times right up to the present, reflects the deep fascination people have for these beautifully bizarre plants.

Cultivation

Introduction

The largest single mistake made by inexperienced growers of cacti and succulents is forgetting that they are plants, and therefore have similar requirements to other plants: water, food, air, and light. Cacti and succulents are, of course, adapted to fairly extreme conditions but they cannot thrive without these vital elements.

No cacti or succulents grow in a true desert comprising only sand, and where there is no rainfall. Most grow in what is usually described as semi-desert: rainfall occurs for a limited number of months in the year, and other xerophytic shrubs and annual plants are common. Many small cacti and succulents begin life in the shade of these bushes, growing above them when they are large and relatively robust, mature plants.

The soils in such places are usually relatively poor in humus, but are often rich in mineral nutrients, only needing sufficient water to turn them into fertile areas. Many cacti and succulents can grow in wetter areas than their natural habitat, but they are less efficient than their more leafy counterparts and so lose out to the competition.

Many features of cacti and succulents are adapted to absorb and store water from the rainfall when it is present, so that the plants can survive through the dry season. These features include a ribbed stem structure to allow for expansion and contraction and a widespread root system for rapid uptake of water.

Opposite: A collection of cacti and succulents growing on a sunny window sill.

Where to Grow Cacti and Succulents?

Cacti and succulent plants are popular horticultural subjects and are grown in many countries over an enormous range of climatic conditions. We know of collectors growing them in places as far apart as Alaska and Singapore.

Indoors

If you have a small number of plants, it is perfectly feasible to grow them indoors. Some groups of succulents adapt much more easily to these conditions than others. The range of plants that can be grown successfully indoors is increased considerably if artificial lighting is used (see page 34). This may be the method you choose, if you live in an area with extreme winter weather where it is not economic to maintain a frost-free greenhouse.

Greenhouse or conservatory

In climates where winter temperatures rarely go lower than 14°F (-10°C), a freestanding greenhouse or conservatory is probably the best choice. The use of cellular plastic materials such as double- or triple-walled polycarbonate, a much better insulator than glass, has extended the practical range of such structures. There is discussion of greenhouses for cacti on page 35. A variant on this idea is the use of heated frames, which can be very effective for globular cacti. A limited range of succulent plants can survive unprotected in these climates and so can be grown outside. The range of such hardy plants may be much larger in very dry areas or if protection from the wet is given in an unheated alpine-style house.

Outside

In favorable climates, where frost is rare, a wide range of succulents can be grown outside. If the amount of rain is particularly heavy, it may be necessary either to modify the soil so it is especially well-draining, or to provide protection in the form of a lathe house. The latter can also be useful in more tropical areas to provide some protection from the sun for those species accustomed to growing under bushes or in more shady areas.

Containers

The variety of containers that can be used for cacti and succulents is wide and, provided the cultivation is suitably adjusted, they do well in most.

Size and shape of plant

Always bear in mind the eventual size and shape of the plant. We are dealing with an enormous range from miniature plants, which will never exceed ½ in. (1.25cm) in diameter, to plants that can grow 40 ft. (12m) tall and weigh several tons.

Small plastic or ceramic pots

The smaller plants will do well in small plastic or glazed ceramic pots.

Shallower pans

Large clumping plants may prefer shallower pans, which will allow them to spread sideways.

Long toms

Certain plants, those that develop deep tap roots, may be better suited to long toms. Long-tom pots are very tall or deep pots, sometimes referred to as Rose pots by garden centers.

Full-depth pots

Larger-growing plants need full-depth pots, and fairly regular repotting for optimum growth. Some of the larger plants respond quite spectacularly to growing in free-root-run conditions.

Small pots

The smaller plants, those that grow naturally in rock crevices, are more successful in cultivation when grown in fairly small pots.

Drainage

It is much safer for those inexperienced in growing cacti and succulents to grow them in containers with one or more drainage holes. Without the drainage hole, watering must be exactly correct. Remember that larger containers take much longer to dry out after watering than small ones, and this has implications for the soil and watering (see page 31). Some species of cacti and succulents, those that naturally occur in very arid regions, are particularly sensitive to their roots becoming waterlogged for too long. Grow these plants in porous clay containers, as they will dry out more quickly. Remember, the larger the container, the more important this is.

Above: A collection of cacti and succulents in decorative containers as they might appear in a greenhouse or on a patio.

Opposite: Porous clay pots are very suitable for growing cacti and succulents.

Right: A globular *Ferocactus chrysacanthus* in a clay pot.

Soil

The type of soil suitable for cacti and succulents is a source of endless debate: there are almost as many soil recipes as there are growers. In our experience, we have used many different types over the years and found it possible to grow good plants, particularly of the easier species, in many different types of soil.

Function of the soil

The soil must provide mechanical support for the plant as well as being a source of water and food.

Peat-based mixtures

Plants from garden centers and other wholesale sources are frequently grown in peat-based mixtures. The reason for this is partly because young plants grow quickly in this medium, and also the soil is light for transport and simplifies mechanical handling at the nursery. The slightly acid reaction of the soil is particularly suitable for some of the South-American cacti such as Notocactus and Gymnocalycium. The food in such composts is used up fairly rapidly, so it is important to use a soluble food at regular intervals. The food should be high in potash and phosphorus and low in nitrogen.

Otherwise there is a tendency for the plant's growth to be rather soft. This leads to a susceptibility to pests and diseases and encourages vegetative growth at the expense of flowering.

Peat-based soils

Peat-based soils are particularly suitable for the epiphytic cacti such as the epiphyllums and Christmas Cacti (*Schlumbergera*). Some growers report good results with adding water-retaining gel crystals, which are available in the horticultural trade for this group of plants.

Many cacti and succulents are rather long-lived, slow-growing plants and therefore may easily be kept in the same container with the same compost for a considerable period of time.

At times when the plants are not frequently watered, the use of peat-based soils can lead to problems. The first problem occurs when a peat-based soil is completely dried out, for it can be difficult to rewet. This can be overcome to a certain extent by adding a small amount of a wetting agent such as a detergent, to the first watering after the rest period. The second problem occurs after a period of a few years when the peat tends to break down, resulting in a change of structure in the soil. It is believed that this breakdown produces chemicals that have a damaging effect on the roots of certain species of cacti,

particularly those from drier areas, which are often regarded as more difficult to grow. To combat this effect, plants in peat-based composts need to be repotted fairly regularly.

Soil-based composts

Many growers use various types of soil-based composts. In some areas John Innes formulation composts are available. They are frequently mixed with coarse sand or gravel to produce a better drained mix. The key to a good compost is to provide one that has a large capacity for absorbing water and chemical nutrients without becoming waterlogged. Materials with very high porosity, such as ground pumice, are very much favored where available. Artificial substitutes such as perlite have been used with considerable success.

These types of compost have a fertilizer content that will last longer than that of a peat-based compost, perhaps up to six months, but they will eventually require additional feeding. We have had good results with granular slow-release fertilizers added to the compost. Slow release fertilizers have a greater duration in cactus and succulent soils as the plants do not absorb the food as quickly as garden annuals, partly because they do not

grow as fast and are not watered so frequently or heavily. It may continue providing food for up to 18 months. Depending on the sources of materials, plants kept in the same containers for many years may well be-come deficient in some trace growth elements. This may show up as chlorosis, weak, poor, or distorted growth. Occasional use of a fertilizer containing trace elements should prevent this from happening.

Some groups of succulents, such as the mesembs, are used to a rather fine-grained, almost clay-like, fairly compacted soil in their native habitat. In cultivation these plants do not grow very well in very loose peat-based composts, preferring a finer-grained soil-based one.

Hydroponic systems

Surprisingly, considering we are dealing with plants adapted to survive periods without water, a few growers have been successful with growing cacti in a hydroponic, or soilless, system. There are technical difficulties, in part arising from the mechanical support needed by heavy plants, and such experiments should be undertaken only after advice from someone with experience of this form of cultivation.

Watering

One of the most frequently asked questions and one of the most difficult to answer is when should I water my plants? Because cacti and succulents do not wilt like other plants there is no automatic visual indicator. Also because there are so many variables such as temperature, size of pot, type of soil, rapidity of plant growth, and type of plant, there can be no easy formula such as "once a week" or "once a month."

In general, these plants will do best if they are almost left to dry out completely between waterings. This might be daily for plants in small pots in a hot greenhouse that are growing well. But large plants in big pots in cooler weather may need watering only once every three or four weeks. This is why a well-drained open compost is so important: it leaves a much wider margin for error in watering.

Right: Xerophyte cacti will show signs of water stress very quickly.

Below: Three methods of watering cacti and succulents.

Over watering will result in splitting or, even worse, rotting.

Points to consider when watering:

• Small pots dry out more quickly than large ones.
• Porous pots dry out much more quickly than plastic or glazed ones.
• Plants in active growth use much more water than those not growing.
• Plants grown in areas where the climate is hot, and humidity low, dry out more quickly than those in a cool, humid climate. (This may include plants grown in a centrally heated environment.)
• Succulents with a large leaf area use much more water than highly succulent species without leaves. Most cacti and succulents are used to a long dormant spell. In most cases this corresponds to a colder, darker winter period; however some plants from southern hemisphere habitats will not change their growing season, growing during the northern hemisphere winter.
• Plants stop growing if short of water, but may rot if overwatered. If in doubt,

it is safer to err on the side of underwatering. If small pots dry out quickly, it may be useful to plunge them on a gravel tray.
• If pots are staying too wet for too long, it may be necessary to apply more artificial heat: this decreases the relative humidity and stimulates water uptake by the plants.

Some growers water their plants carefully, making sure that no water gets on the stem. While this might be important under poor growing conditions, it is not necessary when the plants are in full growth. From time to time we do use a hose in the greenhouse to give everything a thorough drenching. It also has the merit of removing dust and cobwebs. Mist spraying of some species can also be beneficial; indeed some genera such as the genus *Copiapoa* obtain most of their moisture from coastal mists in their native habitats in Chile.

Repotting

When to repot

Soil in a pot eventually becomes exhausted and needs to be replaced.

A plant may have outgrown its container and requires a larger one.

If we suspect that something is wrong with a plant, we will repot it to have a good look at its roots in search of the problem.

Handling cacti

Handling cacti can be tricky for the inexperienced. We have found gloves to be useless: they rapidly become full of spines and as uncomfortable as the cacti itself.

Here are a few tips:
• Hold young plants at the neck where the spines are weak or nonexistent.
• Hold the plant by its root ball, if the rootball is strong.
• Hold plants with fewer, stronger spines between the spines or by the spines, if possible.
• For plants with many uniform spines, it may be possible to actually hold them with little discomfort as the pressure is distributed over many points (the Fakir's-bed principle).
• Manipulate tall plants with a temporary strap made of newspaper, which is then disposable.
• Use broad wooden tongs.
• For very large, heavy spiny plants, wrap them in sheets

2

3

4

1. this mammillaria in a 3½ in. (9cm) pot desperately needs to be repotted.

2. Tip out the plant onto your palm or a wad of newspaper, examining the roots for any problems, i.e., insects or damage.

3. Select a slightly larger pot (about 1 in./2.5cm in diameter larger), cover the bottom with drainage material (broken clay pot shards), put a little of the new compost in the pot, place the plant in position, and fill gaps with new soil.

4. Finally, top dress with fine aquarium gravel. Do not water for at least one week after repotting.

of expanded styrofoam.

• Succulents, with the exception of a few, such as euphorbias, are less problematic.

Watch out for:

• Hooked spined plants: one can get badly entangled in them.

• The genus *Opuntia* and relatives: their barbed spines (glochids) are difficult to remove. We have found the best way to remove them is to apply transparent adhesive tape to your skin (where the spines are stuck in). When the tape is pulled off, it will remove most of these irritant spines.

• The sap of euphorbias: this can be very unpleasant and inflammatory in cuts or other sensitive skin areas. If affected, wash immediately with cold water and seek medical advice.

Indoor Cultivation

Most collectors started out by simply keeping some plants indoors. This can be a successful method of cultivation.

PLANTS FOR INDOOR CULTIVATION

There are some groups of plants that take particularly well to indoor cultivation. They may indeed grow better than they do in a greenhouse. The epiphytic cacti are a good example of this, as are the hoyas, ceropegieas, and sansevierias. Many other plants will grow as well under these conditions as they will in a greenhouse. These include plants of the genera *Rebutia*, *Notocactus*, *Gymnocalycium*, some mammillarias, aloes, haworthias, stapeliads, and some crassulas. Some of the very leafy species of *Euphorbia* are also quite at home indoors.

In countries where winters are extremely severe there may be no option but to keep plants indoors.

For example, in Eastern Europe many collectors use their greenhouses only in the summer, because fuel for heating greenhouses is very expensive or impossible to obtain. In the winter they remove their plants from the pots and store them, wrapped in newspaper, in a cool dry cellar. This technique is surprisingly successful. Some plants, such as opuntias, are best kept in the greenhouse because of the dangers of their glochids and spines.

Artificial lighting

The use of artificial lighting makes it possible to grow almost any succulent plant indoors, with the possible exception of some of the taller-growing species because they are difficult to accommodate and light adequately.

A full discussion of artificial lighting for plants probably is a book in itself, but a few basics need to be mentioned here. Plants make use of light at particular frequencies or "colors," and this must be provided by the artificial lighting you use.

Tungsten bulbs The normal incandescent tungsten bulb provides little light of the right frequency and is more or less useless from the point of view of the plant.

Fluorescent tubes The most commonly used lights for plants are fluorescent tubes. Many types are available, but some have been specifically designed to emit the right colors for plants. Largely developed for the aquarium business, they are also the best type to use for your succulents. They are fairly cheap to run, but it is important

Poor light results in pale, drawn growth, weak spines, and lack of flowers.

to remember that the fluorescent material on the inside of the glass tube starts deteriorating fairly quickly after six months" use, so the tubes must be replaced regularly.

To provide sufficient lighting for succulent plants, use closely spaced tubes. It helps to have good reflectors so that the maximum amount of light is directed toward the plants. Check the amount of heat generated from the tube ballasts or starters to make sure the temperature does not become excessive for the plants. If the fluorescent tubes are kept on a time-switch to control the day length rather than

operated manually, you may need a special circuit breaker as the tubes create a current surge when switched on.

Warning: remember that the combination of electricity and water can be lethal. If you are in doubt about what is involved, consult a professional electrician.

Metal halogen lamps Alternatively, metal halogen lamps, frequently used in commercial greenhouses for plants requiring additional daylight length, can be used. Commercial growers prefer them because they produce much more light for the same amount of energy. The disadvantage is that the equipment needed to run them is expensive, as is the cost of the lamps. For someone contemplating a large set-up, their use is worth investigating.

Watering

On the whole, indoor environments are likely to be warmer and have a drier atmosphere than a greenhouse or some conservatories. As a consequence, the plants may need occasional watering during the winter, particularly in centrally heated rooms.

Greenhouse and Conservatory Cultivation

Greenhouses and conservatories, with their strong light and abundant heat, suit many cacti and succulents.

HEATED GREENHOUSES

A greenhouse is in many ways the best place to grow cacti and succulents because it is designed specifically to give maximum control over the environment.

The more thought you give to each detail of selecting, siting, and constructing your greenhouse will help ensure success in growing cacti and succulents in it.

Size

Most collectors have a very small greenhouse, 8 x 6 ft. (3 x 2m), and this can present particular problems, such as overheating, and lack of air movement. Modern gardens tend to be quite small, which may not leave space for anything larger; however it is possible to have a very interesting collection in a small area. If space is at a premium, choose plants that are going to stay small. Many species of cacti and succulent rarely exceed 3 in. (7.5cm) in diameter.

Site

Selecting the site for your greenhouse, preferably before you buy it, is obviously important. Remember that greenhouses sited with the ridge running east–west receive more light than those with the ridge running north–south.

Base and floor

The base and floor are important. Concrete is best. It helps to keep the moisture down and the light intensity up. Rest the structure on, and secure it to, a course or two of bricks. A dark, earth floor will attract moisture, slugs and snails, moles, mice, and who knows what else. Putting stone slabs down is an easier alternative to concrete, but will still allow many outsiders in.

Cacti and succulents in a typical greenhouse, with aluminum staging and a concrete floor. Adequate light, heat, and ventilation is very important.

Staging the plants

Once the size of the structure is decided, it is equally important to think about arrangements for staging the plants. Different levels of shelves enable plants with differing requirements to be placed appropriately to allow the plants to thrive.

Try to arrange all plants in reachable positions, so a number of other plants will not have to be moved to get to them. When you have run out of space, put up a few hanging shelves to relieve the burden.

We remember once seeing a collection of cacti in a greenhouse, but were unable to figure out where one could walk inside to see the plants. Every part of the floor had staging on it. How did the owner get at them? Did he take the

glass out? It transpired that the final, lowest level of very short plants were on carts which were pushed under the benching as he entered the greenhouse, and pulled out again upon leaving!

Ventilation

If the greenhouse is fairly small, ventilation is going to be critical as a small structure heats up extremely quickly.

Normal greenhouses are sold with too little ventilation for cacti and succulents. Think about adding extra windows or louver vents. An electric extractor fan could be a very beneficial addition.

We do not like our greenhouse going over 105°F (40°C) for any length of time, because this makes the plants go dormant even if it does not damage them. We can usually keep to this by providing enough natural ventilation and the occasional use of forced electric-fan ventilation. If your summers are particularly hot, then it may be necessary to provide some shading.

Heating

Most growers will require some form of heating for their cacti and succulents.
Electric heaters This is by far the easiest form to use. Quite accurate thermostatic controls are available which will minimize the cost. Unlike gas or paraffin (kerosene) heating, no additional water is added to the atmosphere.
Gas or paraffin heaters If this method is used, there must be some ventilation at all times to provide sufficient oxygen supply.
Paraffin (or kerosene) heaters, when allowed to burn with inadequate air, can produce a smoky

This artist's impression of a collection of mostly leaf succulents captures well the variety of hues that these plants display.

flame which can make a terrible mess of the plants. You must make additional water available in the atmosphere. Also, some leafy succulents may be sensitive to sulfurous compounds in the gas supply.
Under-soil heating cables
If you are growing small numbers of more tender succulents, propagators incorporating under-soil heating cables can be a useful facility.

Insulation

Insulation is particularly important for smaller greenhouses. Larger structures are naturally much more stable in temperature, taking longer to heat up and cool down, and in many ways are therefore easier to manage.
Bubble-wrap plastic
Many growers line their greenhouses with bubble-wrap plastic for additional insulation. We believe the disadvantages far outweigh the advantages: it considerably reduces the ventilation and light and also tends to hold condensation inside the greenhouse. If it is used, then choose a horticultural grade of plastic: it is not so rapidly degraded by UV light.
Polycarbonate sheeting
If the local climate is severe in the winter, we recommend replacing the glass with twin- or even triple-wall polycarbonate sheeting. While the thicker grades of this material are quite expensive, it is quite durable and the savings in heating costs will almost certainly outweigh the expense.

Cold Greenhouse

The range of plants that can be grown in a cold greenhouse is naturally somewhat restricted, compared to a structure in which some heat is used.

Plants to avoid Succulent plants originating in East and West Africa, Arabia, southern Mexico, the West Indies, Venezuela, and Brazil should be avoided.

Plants to use Some of the globular cacti are the best subjects for a cold greenhouse, such as echinocereus and lobivias. Within the succulents, some species of agave are among the hardiest. Many South African plants will also withstand temperatures just below freezing for a short period.

FRAMES
This method of cultivation can be very effective for species that do not grow too tall. Use a heating cable to maintain the required minimum temperature in the winter, and ensure that the top of the frame can be removed in summer to give your plants maximum sun and air.

Left: Cactus showing damage caused by cold.

Right: How the sun's rays affect a greenhouse.

Conservatories

Many people have the ideal place in which to grow cacti and succulents: a sunroom or conservatory attached to the house. These plants are perfect for sunrooms and conservatories, which are very often too hot and dry for most other plants.

A difficulty is that such structures often have inadequate or no ventilation. This can be avoided if the structure is designed from scratch, but if adapting an existing structure the simplest solution is to install an extractor fan or two.

In a conservatory it is worthwhile having a bench that allows for the plunging of pots into a coarse, granular, water-retaining material. Such materials are available from garden centers, and are frequently used for other types of plants as well.

Create natural-looking planted beds within your conservatory, where large plants can grow and develop attractively.

If children or animals are likely to use the area, it may be a good idea to restrict the plants you select to the less spiky and less dangerous succulents.

What Is Hardiness?

Hardiness is the ability of a plant to withstand low temperatures or several degrees of frost in the open air.

Many cacti and some succulents certainly can endure quite low temperatures in their natural environments. They may either originate in areas at extreme northern or southern latitudes, or grow naturally at high altitudes. The plants from the extreme latitudes are more likely to prove hardy under most conditions as they are more used to prolonged periods of adverse weather conditions. The high-altitude plants experience extreme swings of conditions, very cold nights and quite intense solar heat during the day as well as very high light intensity. Such changes are not easy to simulate in cultivation.

To avoid disappointment, remember that what is hardy under your own local conditions will vary considerably, depending not only on the minimum temperatures, but also on the rainfall, snow cover, and winter sunshine that your local climate provides.

Hardy Plants

A few succulents are traditionally grown as hardy plants, for they are tolerant of quite severe conditions.

Sempervivum The sempervivums are alpine plants which, if given a well-drained soil, such as on a rock garden, will produce attractive plants that are deservedly popular. A wide range of hybrids is also available.

Agave huachucensis is from Mexico and has beautiful blue leaves and very dark brown, almost black teeth and apical spine.

However, just a few species are not fully hardy, and do need some protection from the wettest weather.

Sedums Sedums are commonly grown as hardy plants. More care is needed with the selection of the species of this genus, as some of the more southerly growing Mexican species are definitely not hardy.

Yucca Some species of yucca are frequently grown as hardy garden plants. There are undoubtedly quite a few species (not commonly available in the horticultural trade), that would also make perfectly hardy and interesting garden plants. There are also quite a few species that,

although they will withstand considerable cold, cannot be used as garden plants because they are very sensitive to excess moisture: the classic example being the Joshua Tree (*Yucca whipplei*) of the Mojave Desert in California.

The yucca commonly sold as a house plant is definitely *not* hardy, except in the most favorable climates, as it comes from largely frost-free areas of Mexico. One of the factors holding back greater horticultural use of yuccas is the lack of good literature on the genus.

Agave We have found some species of agave to be reasonably hardy, taking 5°F (-15°C) of frost even if wet. The most likely cause of damage is frequent freezing/thawing cycles of ice in the centers of the plants. If kept under drier shelter many could undoubtedly survive lower temperatures. A related plant, *Dasylirion wheeleri*, is so far quite happy outside all year, in our experience.

Opuntia erinacea has a dense covering of long white spines and has varieties with pink or yellow flowers.

Opuntia Quite a number of species of *Opuntia* are very hardy, particularly the low-growing species from Canada and the northern United States, such as some forms of *O. fragilis*, *O. polyacantha*, *O. humifusa*, and *O. macrorhiza*. These make good rock-garden plants, producing attractive flower displays in the spring. There is a drawback: the spines and glochids make weeding difficult. However, growers have found that the opuntias are not particularly susceptible to the effects of selective weed killers, so this is a possible method of solving this problem.

Other species of *Opuntia* are tolerant of very cold conditions, but are somewhat more sensitive to excess moisture; *O.basilaris* and *O.erinacea* fall into this category.

Other hardy cacti This sensitivity to excess moisture applies to most other hardy cacti. It includes a number of species of *Echinocereus* such as *E. triglochidiatus*, some northerly occurring forms of *Escobaria vivipara*, *Neobesseya missouriensis*, and *Pediocactus simpsonii*.

A number of plants of the *Mesembryanthemum* will tolerate fairly extreme low temperatures, but only if they are very dry.

Propagation

Seed Raising

Seed raising is the largest single method of propagating cacti and succulents. Seed is available for a wide variety of cacti and succulents, and is cheap when purchased from specialty suppliers. Note: Mixed packets of seed from general garden seed suppliers tend to be rather expensive and the mixture of fast- and slow-growing types makes their cultivation more difficult.

Method

We suggest that you first try out the techniques required on the more robust, quickly growing species. Then progress to those cacti and succulent seedlings that are fairly slow to get established and therefore need more careful care.

Many growers have developed their own favorite methods and it may be necessary for you to experiment a little to find out what works best for you.

Containers

Decide on the kinds of containers you are going to use. If you are growing large numbers of the same sort, then the traditional rectangular seed pan is fine. This is suitable

Cactus fruit showing the seed embedded in a sweet pulp.

for up to 2,000 seeds. If, as is more likely, you have a packet of twenty to thirty seeds, then divide the area of this tray into small squares for each sort. Use small pieces of plastic or glass for the division. Alternatively, small individual pots can be used; small square ones are very convenient.

Soil

For the soil you can use the same compost as for bigger plants, but pass it through a sieve to remove the larger particles. It is also important that the compost is prepared from clean materials free of weed seeds and fungi. It may be useful to sterilize it. After the compost has been put in the containers, they should be placed in a tray of water and allowed to become thoroughly saturated.

Sewing seed

The seed may then be thinly and evenly sprinkled on the surface of the compost. Cover the seeds with a very thin layer of coarse grit. Note: There is one exception to this: the seeds of *Mesembryanthemum,* such as lithops, need light to germinate and should *not* be covered.

Germination

Most seeds germinate best at around 70°F (21°C). It may be necessary to use some artificial heat to reach this temperature, particularly if the seeds are being started early in the year. If it can be arranged, some temperature differential between day and night improves germination. It is necessary to maintain a fairly humid atmosphere while the seeds are germinating. Some growers achieve this by sealing individual pots in plastic bags. Also, trays can be covered with sheets of glass or plastic. Once the seedlings have germinated they can be introduced to the light and more air, although direct sunshine is not a good idea at this stage. Keep them reasonably moist and do not allow them to dry out completely.

When to start seedlings

We recommend that you try to start seedlings fairly early in the year, so they have a reasonably long growing season before their first winter. After six months, faster-growing kinds, particularly some of the succulents, columnar cacti, and opuntias, can be ready for either individual small pots or trays. Slower-growing cacti and succulents can be left in their original containers for up to a year or even more.

Reluctance to germinate

A few types of cacti and succulent seeds can be reluctant to germinate. There are several reasons for this. In some cases, the seed coat may contain germination inhibitors. In other cases, the seed must be a few years old before it will germinate. Another factor can be that cold/heat cycles are needed to prepare the seed for germination.

Pests

If seedlings are troubled with damping-off fungus, watering with a copper-fungicide solution may help. Also, watch out for small black flying insects (Fungus Gnats or Sciarid Fly, see page 52), whose grubs can rapidly destroy pans of seedlings; yellow sticky traps are effective for this.

Labeling

It is important to arrange a good system of labeling, so the individual species can be identified. Since the seeds are so tiny, it may be simplest to give each container or division a numbered tag and maintain an index elsewhere.

Pan of seedlings showing young plants already flowering in their second year.

Cuttings

Many cacti and succulents are readily propagated by cuttings. The process is a little different from rooting cuttings of non-succulent plants, where the chief problem is that the cuttings wilt before they can form roots to absorb water. With cacti and succulents the main difficulty is the danger of fungal rot entering cut surfaces.

To avoid fungal rot

It is therefore important to keep any cut surfaces clean and to allow them to form a dry callous over the wound before placing the cuttings in soil. The length of time this takes to form depends on the area of the cut surface and the temperature and humidity when the cuttings are taken. In most cases, it is best to minimize the cut area by taking stem or shoot cuttings at a narrow point.

Note: The one exception to this is epiphyllum cuttings which root better from a broad cut on the stem. Typically one week to two weeks should be left before planting the cuttings in moist soil.

Large cuttings with a broad area of cut can be left for a month or more. Cuttings that root slowly may benefit from gentle bottom heat. Some leafy succulents can have stem cuttings planted almost immediately. Clumping cacti or spreading succulents may grow roots while still on the parent plants and these can also be potted up much more quickly. For plants very sensitive to rot, a fungicidal powder or flowers of sulfur dusted on the stems can be useful. Hormone rooting powder is not usually necessary but may be useful in a few cases.

Plants to propagate by cuttings

Most mesembs are easily propagated by cuttings, even the very succulent ones such as lithops. However, it is important that a small amount of the woody tissue at the base of the leaves be included in the cutting. Single leaves may occasionally root, but will not form a new meristem (growing point). Single leaves of some other succulents, however, can be propagated by this route. This includes: sansevierias, gasterias, some echeverias, sedums, and pachyphytums. For sanseverias and gasterias even a part of a leaf may root and produce plantlets. The *Echeveria* group needs whole fresh leaves taken cleanly from

Above: Roots forming on a succulent cutting.

Below: Roots forming on a cactus cutting.

the stem or in some cases from the inflorescence.

GRAFTING

Grafting cacti, and to a lesser extent some succulents, is a very useful technique. Grafting can be used for the following purposes: to grow difficult or weakly growing species by placing them on a vigorous rootstock; to keep cristate plants clear of the soil to avoid the dangers of rotting; to force some species into rapid proliferation of offsets, which can then either be grafted again or re-rooted on their own roots as cuttings. Grafting is also the only way of keeping alive the genetic aberrations of completely variegated plants, i.e., those totally lacking chlorophyll.

Plant families to graft

It is important to remember that the technique works only with families belonging to the Dicotyledonous plants (i.e., those having two seedling leaves). Families of plants belonging to the monocotyledonous plants, e.g., Asphodelaceae or Agavaceae, lack the internal structures that make grafting possible. Grafts are very commonly used in the Cactaceae and occasionally in the Euphorbiaceae, Portulaceae, Asclepiadaceae, and Apocynaceae.

Points to note

Grafts between plants of closely related species are more likely to be successful, and the more closely related, the more successful this will be. Indeed, plants of different families rarely make successful grafts.

Grafts are best undertaken when both the stock (the rooted part) and the scion (the top part) are in active growth, probably in the spring or summer. The stock and scion should be of similar diameter and turgidity.

Stock plants

Many species can be used as stock plants, but the genus *Trichocereus* is probably the favorite.

If *Echinopsis* is used, it should not be a species that offsets too freely.

The diagrams illustrate the variety of ways grafting can be achieved and the numerous means of attaching the stock to the scion.

A number of commercial grafts are done on three-ribbed *Hylocereus*; this stock is very vigorous but its high winter temperature requirement often causes problems in amateurs' greenhouses.

Another stock with slightly similar problems, but not quite so demanding, is *Myrtillocactus geometrizans*. It can be recognized by the slightly glaucous six-angled stems.

Specialists in grafting tiny seedlings often recommend *Pereskiopsis*, which can sometimes turn tiny seedlings into flowering plants in a matter of months.

Very vigorous opuntias can sometimes be the best stock for grafting plants of the *Opuntiae* tribe.

Some interesting experiments have also been done recently using *Echinocereus triglochidiatus* as a stock for tricky, cold hardy plants such as some of the pediocacti.

For stapeliads, one of the larger, stronger-growing *Stapelia* species is commonly used, an alternative being *Ceropegiea woodii* tubers.

For the euphorbias, favorites are *E.ingens* or *E.canariensis*.

Method and tools

A good clean sharp knife is an essential tool.

Cut the top off the stock, and then bevel off the edges so that the surface does not become concave when dry. Cut the bottom off the scion, and press together the two cut surfaces. It is important that the vascular bundles of the stock and scion are adjacent as they must unite in order for the flow of water and food to be conducted from the stock to the scion.

Use some method to maintain this pressure for a period of a few weeks while the tissues unite. The most commonly used method is placing two rubber bands around the pot and over the top of the graft, at right angles to each other. Many other ingenious ideas using weights and clips have been suggested. Experiment to find what is convenient and practical for you.

Once the grafts have been made, put them in a warm place, out of direct sunshine and preferably not too dry an atmosphere. It usually takes a couple of weeks for the union to be sufficiently secure for you to release the pressure you have applied.

For some types of plants variants on this flat-grafting technique, such as cutting a V-shaped wedge, can be used. Some possible arrangements are illustrated in the diagram.

Pests and Diseases

Pests

Cacti and succulents, like most plants grown under intensive conditions, can be attacked by a variety of pests. Their fairly tough tissue lessens the risk a little but regular inspection is necessary to avoid problems.

MEALY BUG

Undoubtedly the worst and most persistent problem is the woolly aphid or mealy bug. They are similar in appearance to small wood-lice, with a white woolly coating, which is waxy, offering protection to the pest.

While most other pests may damage plants, this one is capable of killing large specimens very rapidly. There are several reasons why mealy bug is particularly dangerous. It breeds very rapidly, consequently attaining large numbers, while also quickly acquiring resistance to pesticides. It seems to be able to lay dormant on inert material for considerable periods of time, then break out when conditions become favorable. Its waxy and woolly covering can make it difficult for contact insecticides to penetrate to the insect. In addition, there are many species of mealy bugs, all of which have slightly different characteristics and habits that further compound the problem.

One of the most persistent pests of cacti and succulents is the mealy bug, also known as the woolly aphid.

Control

Systemic insecticide The normal way of attacking the mealy bug is to use a systemic insecticide, usually one based on an organophosphorus compound. While these can be quite effective, many strains of mealy bug have built up some resistance to them, and it may be necessary to try more than one type for effective control. However, this has been made more difficult by the fact that some of the most effective types are no longer available on the market, because of the more expensive testing now required for market approval. Due to this wide variability in what is available in different markets, it is not possible to recommend specific chemicals. Check what is available locally.

Washing away For some plants it is possible to wash away the bugs in a jet of water, perhaps with some wetting agent. With small infections it may be possible to squash or otherwise physically remove the bugs, which look like small woolly lumps. Some growers use methyl alcohol or other forms of alcohol to dab on the insects which removes their waxing coatings and definitely kills them; however, you could damage the plants themselves by using the alcohol.

Nicotine solution An old gardeners' remedy was to accumulate cigarette butts in water: the resulting nicotine solution was used to kill the bugs. Such homemade remedies are now illegal in many countries, and also carry dangers of transmission of tobacco mosaic virus to susceptible plants.

Biological controls Biological control methods are favored over the use of insecticides. These methods are often used successfully on the commercial scale, but it is not easy to use the technique on small, personal collections.

Several predators for mealy bugs can be purchased from commercial sources, including

lacewings and species of Cryptolaemus, which is related to the ladybug. Both will also help to control other aphid-related pests, such as scale, green fly, and white fly. If you have a particularly bad attack of mealy bug, they may be worth considering.

Drawbacks of biological control include: Insecticides can no longer be used for any other pests, so you may need biological controls for them, too.

Some of the pest must always be available, otherwise the predators will starve or go elsewhere. To survive, many of the predators need somewhat higher temperatures than are often maintained in amateurs' cacti-and-succulent greenhouses.

Prevention It is easier to keep mealy bug out of a collection of cacti and succulents than to control it once it is in; so it is a very good idea to quarantine new plants to make sure that they are not introducing pests. If mealy bugs appear, it is vital to deal with them right away before they have a chance to multiply. Good hygiene is important as mealy bugs love to hide under dead leaves or flowers and other places where you and your insecticide spray cannot reach.

Root attacks One particular species of mealy bug attacks the roots of cacti. This form is seen as white patches on the roots when repotting a plant. If a plant is unaccountably sick and not growing, take it out of its pot and examine the roots. If the bugs are found, wash off all the soil and bugs in a jet of water, allow to dry, and repot in fresh clean soil.

Damage to a cactus done by the red spider mite.

RED SPIDER MITE

Red spider mite is on the whole less of a problem than mealy bug. These creatures are not actually spiders (do not confuse them with the much larger red sand spiders often seen on dry-stone walls and quite harmless to plants), but actually a parasitic mite, reddish-orange in color. The worst feature is that the mites are very small, in fact almost invisible, so that unless you have particularly good eyesight, the damage may be the first thing that you do see. This usually appears as brown scarring on the younger growth.

Susceptible plants

Only the minority of cacti and succulents are susceptible. Among the cacti, rebutias, lobivias, and coryphanthas are most commonly attacked, but it will occasionally also go for melocactus, sulcorebutia, some mamillarias, and some of the smaller mexican globular cacti such as lophophora, turbinicarpus, and pelecyphora.

Some of the Mesembryanthemaceae, for example faucarias, are also prone to red-spider-mite attack. We believe this may be a different species, as the mites appear black rather than red as in the case of the ones found on cacti. However, the damage and recommended treatment are the same.

Certain species of caudiciform succulents are also very prone to similar mite attack on the leaves of their annual vines. Again, this is certainly not the same as the cactus species pest, and may be different from those attacking the mesembs.

Prevention and Control

The pest is encouraged by hot, dry conditions and lack of adequate ventilation. We have found that a more humid atmosphere on its own is insufficient to prevent recurrence, but when combined with the maximum ventilation the problem is quite rare.

Persistent use of appropriate chemicals can kill the pests (check what is available at your local garden center).

We recommend that you be particularly vigilant for this pest if you have a nearby hedge of *Chamaecyparis leylandii*, which can harbor the pest over winter.

SCALE INSECTS

This relatively uncommon sap-feeding pest is brown or grayish-brown in color. It is most often seen on agaves and opuntias.

Control

Direct spraying with insecticide is not very effective because the insects have a hard, impenetrable shell-like coating. A systemic insecticide that the pests will suck from the plants can be more effective. Sometimes hand removal can be fairly easy and effective.

WESTERN FLOWER THRIPS

This is a new pest to cacti and succulents. These small, fast-moving insects range in color from lemon-yellow to dusky yellow-brown. They are often seen in the flowers, where they can cause distortion of the flowers and lack of fertility, but are unlikely to actually harm the plants.

Control

They are best controlled with sticky traps.

Scale insets on a yucca. This sap-eating pest is fortunately not very common.

SLUGS AND SNAILS

These mollusks can be a problem, particularly on the more fleshy succulents.

Prevention and Control

Greenhouse hygiene is important. Remember, locating the offenders is far more successful at night when they are active. In extreme cases it may be necessary to use slug bait.

ANTS

Ants do not actually damage the plants themselves but may introduce mealy bugs or other aphids. In extreme cases nest-building activity may upset roots.

Control

If necessary use a powdered insecticide.

LEAF CUTTER BEES

These often solitary bees are hairy, and black or metallic blue, green, or purple. They have been an annoying pest in our greenhouses for many years. They excavate tunnels in pots where they lay their eggs in carefully constructed leaf-lined cells. This can cause two problems: first, the leaves can initiate rotting of the plant roots; and second, if a large tap root gets in the way the bees are quite capable of boring a large hole straight though it. Leaf cutter bees are particularly fond of hanging baskets, which provide an attractive warm dry spot for this egg-laying activity.

Control

The remedy is to repot the plants, removing the leaf-lined cells as soon as this activity is spotted.

SCIARID FLY (Mushroom Flies or Fungus Gnats)

These tiny flies, sooty-gray to black in color, produce grubs that can cause problems. The small, white grubs are rarely a danger to larger plants but can do serious damage to the roots of very young seedlings. The pest is associated almost exclusively with peat-based composts.

Control

Yellow sticky insecticidal strips are very effective for trapping the adult flies, thus breaking the breeding cycle.

EELWORM OR NEMATODE

Eelworms are microscopic, transparent worm-like creatures. This pest seems largely confined to relatively warm areas, and we have fortunately never seen it. The creatures cause large cyst-like growths on the roots which then cause stunting of the plants.

Control

Normal insecticides are not very effective. The usually recommended treatment is to put the plant in water at 122°F (50°C) for 15 to 20 minutes. There are effective chemical treatments available only to commercial growers.

TORTRIX MOTH CATERPILLAR

These caterpillars are an occasional problem with leafy succulents or mesembs.

If some leaves appear stuck together with a cocoon, pry them open and you may find a small grub eating the leaves.

Control

Removal by hand is adequate control.

VINE WEEVIL

Vine weevils are slow moving black beetles just under ½ in. long, with pale brown flecks on their wings. This pest can attack a limited number of succulent genera. Echeverias are the most susceptible, and occasionally aeoniums. The first sign is usually the collapse of the stem.

Control

If the stem is hollow with grubs inside, cut back the stem to a sound area. Then treat the plant as a cutting and plant in clean fresh soil, and incinerate the infected plant material.

GREEN FLY

Green fly is not usually a problem on cacti and succulents, although we have experienced it on the flower spikes of aloes and haworthias.

Control

The usual chemical sprays are effective, or simply remove and destroy the flower spikes.

WHITE FLY

White fly leaves most cacti and succulents alone, but we have had troublesome outbreaks on leafy caudiciform succulents or succulent pelargoniums.

Control

Yellow sticky insecticidal strips help control white fly. The problem will eventually correct itself during the dormant period, when the plant has no leaves and is being kept cool.

Green fly, seen here on a leafy succulent, usually affect only the flower spikes of particular plants.

Diseases

Cacti and succulents are susceptible to two groups of diseases: the fungal and bacterial rots, and those diseases caused by mineral deficiencies in the soil.

ROTTING

The main diseases of cacti and succulent plants are due to various fungal and bacterial rots. In general, healthy, growing plants are fortunately quite able to resist these infections.

Causes

They commonly occur as a secondary effect of other problems, such as attack by insects, pests, physical damage leaving exposed plant tissue, or incorrect growing conditions. The single biggest cause probably occurs when fungal rots enter via dead roots, which result from poor root aeration.

Prevention and Control

The best way to avoid these problems is to provide conditions that prevent their development, i.e., a healthy pest-free environment. Look for discolored vascular tissue which may be red or brown and penetrate some way into otherwise healthy tissue.

Cut away diseased tissue If they occur and are spotted early, it may be possible to save the plant by cutting away all the diseased tissue with a clean knife; first clean the knife with alcohol to prevent spreading fungal spores. It may be beneficial to dust the cut surfaces with flowers of sulfur.

Fungicidal chemicals They can give some protection, but use this only as a last resort, since they are not effective against the whole range of different rot-producing fungi.

Copper fungicides Young cactus and succulent seedlings are particularly prone to "damping off," which is a fungal attack. This can be partially controlled by copper fungicides. The other frequently mentioned chemical for this purpose, "chinosol," is suspected of causing some damage to the seedlings and is not recommended.

Deficiency Diseases

The other group of diseases affecting succulent plants are caused by soil deficiencies of various minerals.

Causes

The cause may not be simply that the soil does not contain the required elements. The minerals may not be available as a result of watering: the soil may have become too alkaline, caused by the build-up of salts from minerals contained in the water used for the plants.

Prevention

Find out the alkalinity of your local water, and if necessary take steps to correct it by adding suitable acid. Unless you are a chemist and have the necessary knowledge, it is inadvisable to use strong mineral acids for this purpose. It is possible to use citric acid or acetic acid (vinegar), but our favorite remedy is potassium dihydrogen phosphate, which also supplies useful elements. If your local rainwater is sufficiently clean then this is the best way to avoid the soil becoming alkaline.

Control

Deficiency diseases are more likely to show up in peat-based rather than soil-based composts. If a plant looks chlorotic or refuses to grow properly, try fresh compost to see if this solves the problem. It may be beneficial to add appropriate supplements, if locally available soils are known to have particular deficiency problems.

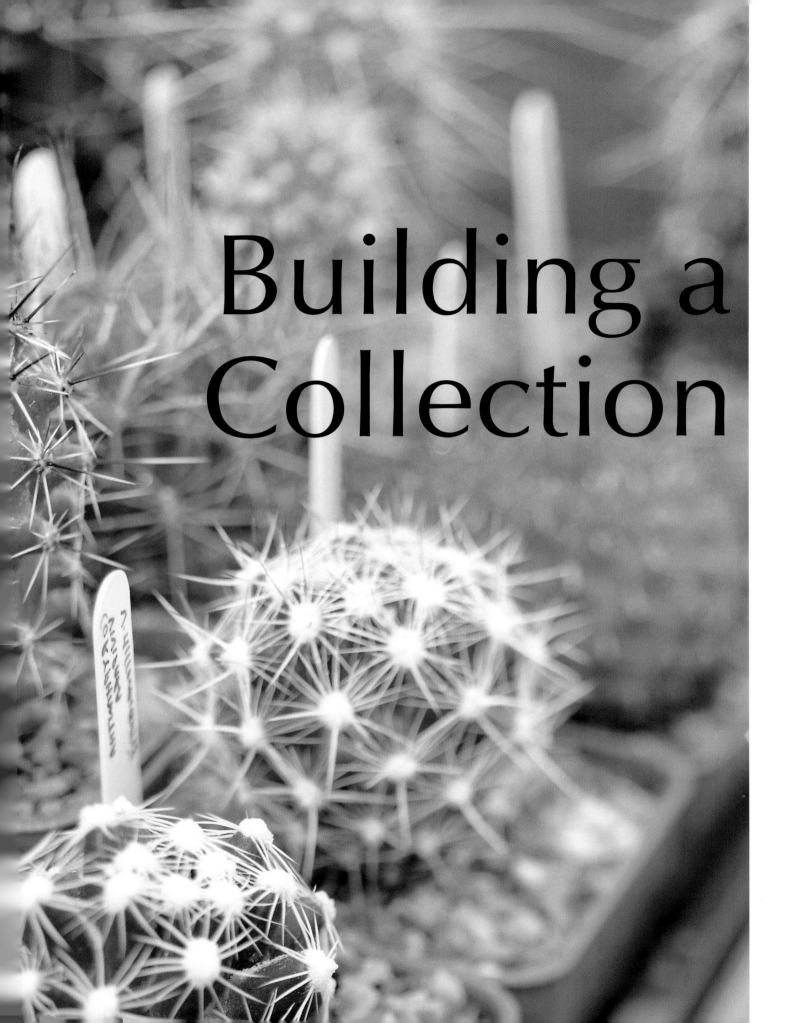

Building a Collection

Creating your own collection of cacti and succulents, whether through purchases, by growing your own from seed, or both, gives great satisfaction. In your own home you can appreciate the diversity and unique features of these exotic plants.

Garden Centers and Florists

For most people, it is likely that your first plants will have been acquired from a garden center or florist. Many of these places have a good selection of plants for sale.

Regrettably, however, such establishments often know little about the care of cacti and succulents. Usually when the plants arrive from the wholesaler they are in good condition. Subsequently, the plants are often displayed in the darkest part of the greenhouse or shop and they are then incorrectly watered (either too much or too little). One result may be infestation with pests, particularly mealy bug. It is also not unknown for dead plants to be left on display.

If you are regular visitor to garden centers and florists, keep a look out for new deliveries of plants which you can be more confident are in good condition. The plants should have a good uniform appearance with bright colors and not show signs of etiolation. Watch for telltale signs of mealy bug: little white woolly lumps.

Warning: If the plants are in flower that is probably a good sign, but watch out for the trick some wholesalers play of sticking on individual, artificial, or dried flowers with glue or pins, which almost certainly will have damaged the plants. Remember most cactus and succulent flowers are short lived, so if your cactus is apparently in flower for several weeks, look closely; you may find they are artificial. Various cacti and succulent societies have tried to eliminate this practice, but in reality there is not a lot that can be done unless the plants are described as "flowering cacti," in which case the trader may be in breach of trade description legislation.

Specialty Nurseries

As you gain more experience you are likely to want to buy specific species that are not commonly available. The specialty nurseries are by far the best source: they have a good range of plants that are usually available at reasonable prices. If you have a nursery in your area, visit it to get good advice as well as good plants.

Should your area not have a specialty nursery, do not worry. Most run a good mail-order service. Fortunately, cacti and succulents are well-suited to the mail-order business: they do not wilt in transit, are often quite compact and reasonably robust.

A densely packed display of tall-growing cacti in the authors' collection.

Growing from Seed

One of the best ways to build up a collection, and for very little expenditure, is to grow the plants from seed. A number of specialty seed suppliers worldwide offer an enormous range. With only a few exceptions, cactus and succulent seed has long viability, and with a little practice results can be very good. Seedling plants you have raised are a source of particular pleasure, and happily often seem to adapt better to your conditions.

You will find that, even though the commercial suppliers have a very good range of plants, there are still many species that are unobtainable. The reasons are that they may not be in cultivation, but more likely there is a low demand for them or they are particularly awkward to propagate. The only way to obtain such plants is through the network of collectors who grow them; find them through joining some of the national and international groups mentioned in the information directory (see page 123).

In our experience, most collectors are only too happy to spare cuttings or seeds of unusual plants to propagate them. In many ways this acts as an insurance against the loss of a plant; on many occasions we have been able to reacquire a rare plant we have lost because we had given away cuttings to other collectors.

From time to time large collections of mature plants come up for sale through a collector who is unable to look after them any longer. This can be a source of valuable mature plants, and such plants do not usually sell for particularly high prices. However, taking on mature specimens that have adapted to their previous owners' conditions may sometimes be tricky and is best undertaken by enthusiasts with some experience.

As your collection grows, so will your knowledge of a range of these intriguing plants, which for the most part are easy to care for, and reward you through their unusual beauty.

It is advisable not to place orders in the depth of winter as the plants may be too cold in transit.

Remember, there may be complications if you want to buy plants from nurseries in other countries, as there may be requirements for import/export licenses and phytosanitary certificates.

You can locate these nurseries through advertisements in the cactus and succulent journals published by the various National Cactus Societies or if you have Internet access, through the Cactus and Succulent Plant Mall (see the information directory on page 123).

A selection of young cactus seedlings on display at a garden center.

Plant Directory

Cacti

Aporocactus

Commonly known as the rat-tail cactus, *Aporocactus flagelliformis* is one of those plants frequently grown by people who do not specialize in cacti. There are good reasons for this: it has been in cultivation a long time, takes a lot of neglect, and will grow well indoors on a sunny window sill. It also makes a good hanging-basket plant with long cylindrical trailing stems that can reach several feet in length. This plant flowers easily in the spring, producing a host of pink flowers. A lot of work has been done in creating hybrids of this species that produce larger flowers of slightly different colors.

Ariocarpus

This small genus of very slow-growing cacti comes from northern Mexico and southern United States. Because they are slow growing and do not get very large, they have been much prized by collectors. In the past, many plants have been taken from their habitats for sale in the horticultural trade. Fortunately, this is no longer the case as the

plants are protected and removal of such plants is now illegal. Seed from plants in cultivation is obtainable fairly easily, and although considerable patience is required it is perfectly possible to raise them by this route. They are not particularly difficult to grow, but some care is needed with their watering. We find it preferable to grow them in clay pots. They have a growing season later in the year than some cacti, flowering usually around September. When they are actually growing and flowering they can take quite heavy watering.

This *Ariocarpus fissuratus* has been grown from seed and is about ten years old.

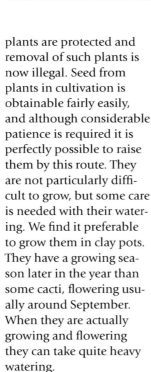

A. kotschoubeyanus, a somewhat smaller, flatter plant is slower growing, but quite easy and will flower at a small size. It grows on flat sandy plains and is reported to be sometimes covered in water for a short period in the rainy season. *A. trigonus*, which, like *A. furfuraceus*, grows on rocky scree slopes, we find to be the most difficult species. The miniature species *A.agavoides* and *A.scapharostris* are both very scarce in the wild as they have been found only in one very small locale.

Fortunately, both are readily available as cultivated seedling grown plants. *A. agavoides* can flower when less than 1 in. (2.5cm) in diameter. Note: They cannot be recommended for indoor cultivation, as very good light is essential.

Arrojadoa

This is a small genus of rather interesting Brazilian cacti, which make small clumps of shrubby stems up to 2–3 ft. (0.60–1m) tall. The characteristic of the genus is that they develop small tufts of bristles and hairs at the tip of the stems from which the small, waxy and usually pink flowers develop. They are quite easy to grow, provided they are given minimum winter temperature that is a little higher than the average, say 50°F (10°C). They grow fairly rapidly and can be expected to flower in three to four years from seed and certainly when they are less than 1 ft. (30.5cm) high.

The thicker-stemmed species such as *Arrojaoda rhodantha* or *A. aureispina* are the most robust while the thinner-stemmed species such as *A. eriocaulis* or *A. penicillata* may need a small amount of winter water to prevent the stems from drying up. They are likely to be found only in a few specialty nurseries.

Astrophytum

This very distinct genus of globular cacti occurs in southern United States and northern Mexico. The astrophytums are distinguished by having a white "speckling" on the epidermis. Because of this feature, their distinctive form, and attractive yellow flowers, they are very popular with collectors. While not suitable for indoor cultivation, they are not difficult to grow under the right conditions. We have found a well-drained mineral-based compost to be

essential. A very sunny position is advised. They are quite cold tolerant and will not be harmed by near-freezing temperatures if dry.

There are only a few species, but these come in a host of variations; also, many hybrids and cultivars have been produced, so it is possible to collect quite a large number of "different" plants. Astrophytums are usually solitary stemmed, branching only if the growing point has been damaged. The largest growing and perhaps the easiest to cultivate is *Astrophytum ornatum*. It can grow to 3 ft. (100cm) or more in height and 6–8 in. (15–20cm) in diameter, however it will take many years to reach this size. As a younger plant this is globular and can be expected to flower at around five to six years old and 3 in. (7.5cm) in diameter. Perhaps the most common species is *A. myriostigma*, sometimes known as the Bishop's Hat cactus because of its shape. This is smaller than *A. ornatum* and lacks spines, it will also start flowering when smaller. The species is quite variable in the wild and a number of different forms are in cultivation.

Astrophytum capricorne is even more variable and slightly more difficult in cultivation.

A. capricorne's main characteristic is a dense "birds-nest" array of flexible, twisted spines over the plant body. These are variable in color and density, as is the spotting on the stem. The flower is probably the best of the genus, being larger and usually having a red center in a yellow flower. Success with it is more difficult because it is somewhat prone to root loss if it is kept too wet and it can then be difficult to re-establish.

A. asterias is another spineless *Astrophytum* which has a form very reminiscent of a sea urchin. This is rather slower growing than the other species and also needs care to avoid overwatering. We struggled to grow a good specimen of this species for some years; then we reverted to growing it in a porous clay pot which has proved much more successful. This is a species more likely to be found only at a specialty nursery.

Left:
Carnegia gigantea, although frequently seen as seedling plants, it is not very successful outside its native area because to grow well it needs much heat and a lot of root room.

Below: Specimen of *Cereus peruvianus f. monstrous*. This is one of the unusual growth forms (see page 15).

Carnegiea

This genus contains only one species, *Carnegiea gigantea*. It is the giant columnar cactus that grows mainly in southern Arizona and adjacent areas of Mexico. It eventually reaches more than 40 ft. (12.25m) in height, and weighs several tons. It is very slow growing and the largest plants are probably 200 to 300 years old. Flowering does not commence until the plants are several feet high, which may take some forty years, even under favorable conditions.

Cephalocerus

This genus used to contain many species, but most have been transferred to other genera within recent years. The remaining species *Cephalocereus senilis* is commonly known as the old man cactus because of its long flexible whiskery spines. It is attractive as a seedling and easy to grow, if a somewhat slow grower. It is very commonly available as seedlings in garden centers. The plants come from an area in the state of Hidalgo in Mexico called the Barranca de Metitzlan. This particular large valley has a very rich cactus flora containing very many beautiful cactus species growing in natural rock gardens. Here the *C. senilis* grow to impressive plants more than 20 ft. (6m) tall. They will not flower until they are large plants, at least 8 ft. (2.5m) in height, so do not expect this to happen in pot culture.

Cereus

These are mostly very fast-growing and robust plants. Many rapidly get too large for the average greenhouse, and in fact will not flower until they are quite large. However, a couple of species are worth looking for because they start to flower at under 3 ft. (100cm) in height. Both come from the Brazilian/Argentinean border and grow happily in normal greenhouse conditions. *C. chalybaeus* has slate-blue stems and short black spines. The flowers are nocturnal, white with a pinkish tube and about 6 in. (15cm) long and 4 in. (10cm) in diameter. They have a delicate perfume. *C. azureus* is more slender and its larger flowers are not produced in quite such profusion.

Cleistocactus

This interesting group of columnar cacti of very easy cultivation deserves to be more widely grown. They can grow very quickly under favorable conditions and many species will flower prolifically. Because they are large, quickly growing cacti, they appreciate plenty of water and frequent doses of fertilizer. Large pots or a free root run are needed with only a relatively short dormant dry spell in the winter. They originate in Andean valleys in Peru and Bolivia. They are tolerant of quite low temperatures, certainly down to freezing, although probably not below this without sustaining some damage.

The most commonly seen species, *Cleistocactus strausii*, which is covered in dense white spines, is certainly eye-catching but is not quite so freely flowering as some other species. To flower it needs to grow a little larger (18 in./

46cm) high and to be in good light. The flowers are a dusky red and long and tubular in shape. Like all the species of *Cleistocactus* they are pollinated by hummingbirds.

Other recommended species include *Cleistocactus flavescens* (yellow flowered), *C. brookei* (red flowered), and *C. vulpiscauda* (also red flowered and very softly spined—the name means fox's tail, and unlike most cacti it can be stroked with impunity). These will all flower at around 9 in. (23cm) tall. Also recommended are *C.dependens* and some of the forms of *C.baumannii*.

Copiapoa

From the dry coastal deserts of northern Chile, this is a group of very interesting globular cacti. There they get much of their moisture from the frequent coastal mists, many receiving little direct rainfall. They are slow growing eventually forming large "barrels" or clumps that must be over 100 years in age.

Surprisingly, they take quite well to cultivation although most species remain slow growing and some will not start flowering until between ten and twenty years old. They prefer a mineral-based soil without a great deal of humus in it. In hot climates it is very important to give them plenty of ventilation as it is surprisingly easy to scorch them. Periodic mist spraying is beneficial. The flowers are all rather similar—yellow and between 1–2 in. (2.5–5cm) in diameter.

The rather softer-bodied species such as *Copiapoa humilis* are the fastest growing and will commence flowering when around four years old from seed. Some of the very stoutly spined species such as *C.cinerea* are quite slow and may need to be twelve to fifteen years old before they will start flowering. With age some develop interesting body colors; for example, *C. cinerea* becomes chalky white.

Coryphantha

This group of mostly fairly small globular cacti comes from northern Mexico and southern United States. They are not particularly difficult to grow, although for best results they do prefer good sunny and light conditions, so they are probably not too suitable for indoor cultivation. Most species have strong spines and are quite attractive even when not in flower. The majority have yellow flowers which are borne at the crown of the plant around midsummer; a few have pink flowers. While some

Copiapoa humilis is one of the faster growing of this genus, and will start flowering when they are four years old from seed.

species remain solitary and will not grow more than 2–3 in. (5–7.5cm) in diameter, some species offset and produce clumps with large numbers of heads. A characteristic of the genus is that the spine clusters and areoles are borne at the tips of tubercles which are separated and do not form ribs. The flowers come from a grove in the top of the tubercle, which is connected to the areole.

One of the most common and easiest to grow species is *Coryphantha bumamma*. This has broad, glossy dark green tubercles and clear, yellow flowers about 2 in. (5cm) in diameter. It can form quite large clumps with age. Much smaller are plants like *C. radians*, which has a dense covering of yellow radial spines, and rarely offsets. The flower is again yellow.

Some species such as *C. erecta* form clusters of more elongated stems; this one is more reluctant to flower in cultivation requiring very sunny conditions. There are a few rarer species such as *C. macromeris* and *C. scheeri* which are a little more difficult in cultivation. They require more careful watering and perhaps little humus in the soil.

Echinocactus

From Mexico and the southern United States, this is a small group of barrel cacti. The best known plant in cultivation is *Echinocactus grusonii*, often called the golden barrel, or more unkindly, mother-in-law's chair. It is a beautiful plant and one that has adapted well to cultivation. This is just as well because it is relatively rare in the wild, being somewhat localized in an area of Mexico where there is now a hydro-electric power plant. This cactus is grown in huge numbers by the wholesale cactus nurseries and is frequently seen in garden centers. Larger plants are grown outside in the southern United States and for the European market in places such as Tenerife and Israel. This is one of those plants that will tolerate a lot of abuse in cultivation and still survive. Under ideal conditions it grows quite quickly and can eventually reach several feet in diameter and height. Flowers, rather small and insignificant, are produced only on fairly old plants, under good conditions.

E. grusonii, under dry conditions, is reported to survive mild frosts, but generally in damper climates it is recommended to keep it a little above freezing or the epidermis can be marked.

Less common in cultivation but more widespread in the wild is *E. ingens*. This species is less tolerant of maltreatment but forms magnificent large barrels in habitat and can also be grown into fine specimens in cultivation. In pot culture it remains very slow and seems to respond best to the free root run conditions in an open bed.

The range of *Echinocactus horizonthalonius* spreads up into the Big Bend National Park area of Texas, as well as into Mexico. It is a much smaller-growing species but is not a plant for the beginner. It needs a light touch: very careful watering, very little humus in the compost, and a very sunny and light position in the greenhouse. This is a species we find worth growing in a clay rather than a plastic pot so that it dries out quickly after watering. It is well worth the effort as the body is a grayish-blue and the very pretty pink flowers appear on quite small plants.

E. texensis (formerly *Homalocephala texensis*) is a plant of a similar nature to the previous species, but probably a little easier to cultivate. It is known locally as the horse crippler because of its very sharp, strong spines. There are also some species of *Echinocactus* that occur in the Mojave Desert in Southern California, and the Grand Canyon. These plants form magnificent multiheaded clumps in these very arid areas and are among the most difficult cacti to cultivate. They are rarely seen in cultivation and should be attempted only by experts with ideal conditions.

Echinocereus

This group of low-growing clumping cacti have beautiful, long-lasting flowers, making them very popular with collectors. They come from northern Mexico and the United States, some growing at surprisingly northerly latitudes and quite high altitudes. Because of this, quite a few species are hardy and can be grown outside under the right conditions. The common American name for these plants is the hedgehog cactus. They can be recognized by their very spiny flower tube.

Some species of *Echinocereus* can be reluctant to produce their flowers. The usual reason is that it is important they have their cool (or even cold) dry winter rest period. Keeping them too warm in winter may inhibit flowering. For some species it is also important to have good light conditions, so they are best grown in a greenhouse, conservatory, or frame.

Echinocereus are unusual in that the flower bud develops within the body of the cactus and then bursts through the stem. This can leave a small scar

Opposite: *Echinocatus grusonii*, a barrel cactus, often called the golden barrel.

Below: *Echinocereus* var. *rubrispinus* is a recent discovery with an attractive form and pink flowers.

and, even under favorable conditions, the dead flowers can start a stem rot. It is important, therefore, to remove the dead flowers, particularly in damp weather.

Many species are worth growing, and most of the species have a fair number of local forms, so it is possible to have quite a large collection of this genus. Some of the less spiny Mexican species are among the easiest to grow and flower. *E. knippelianus* grows into small clumps of globular heads and has nice pink flowers in the spring. *E. pulchellus* is similar, but has more ribs and is more spiny. *E. sheerii* is a larger-growing species that forms clumps of more elongated stems. This species and a number of very closely related ones such as *E. salm-dykianus* and *E. gentryi* have long-tubed flowers that tend to stay open into the evening. They are very easy to grow and flower. Growing at high altitudes in Mexico is the hairy *E. delaetii*. This is much more reluctant to flower in cultivation unless very good light can be provided.

Some species of *Echinocereus* form very large clumps of heads, such as *E. enneacanthus*. They can also be somewhat more reluctant to flower if given too much water, heat, and/or nitrogenous food when they will grow rampantly.

The flowers are worth waiting for, being large and long lasting. *E.pentalophus* is similar with rather straggly unattractive stems but very beautiful flowers. Much neater are the plants sometimes called the Rainbow cactus (*E. pectinatus*) because of its attractive colored spines. These plants occur on both sides of the Mexican/U.S. border and come in a very wide range of forms. A particularly attractive form was discovered about twenty years ago and is usually called *E.* var. *rubrispinus.* The flower is pink and some 4 in. (10cm) in diameter.

Also very attractive and relatively small growing is *E.reichenbachii*, some forms of which grow as far north as Oklahoma and will take quite cold conditions if dry in the winter. The same is true of *E.chloranthus,* which has forms with small greenish or brownish flowers.

E. engelmannii with needle-like spines can also form quite large clumps of very attractive stems. It will withstand quite cold conditions but is not very tolerant of damp. The very large flowers are unusually

beautiful, but will form only if the light conditions are good and if the plant is not kept too warm in winter.

E. triglochidiatus is a very common U.S. species, and occurs in a wide variety of forms. Some grow at surprisingly high altitudes and far north in the United States and are therefore quite hardy. Some forms can form very big clumps and can be quite spectacular when they are in flower in the spring. The rich orange-red flowers are quite large; unlike many cactus flowers, they do

Beautiful large flower typical of the genus *Echinopsis*.

not close up at night. The common name is the claret-cup cactus.

Echinopsis

Plants of the genus *Echinopsis* are very common in cultivation. Many people who have only a few plants will likely have an echinopsis or two. There are very good reasons: they are mostly very easy to grow, take well to indoor cultivation, and will tolerate a lot of bad cultivation and neglect. They are also common because they offset freely and the offsets root very

easily. So, given even moderately good conditions they will flower and, as the flowers are mostly large and sometimes nicely scented, they are much appreciated but rather short-lived. Because they have been in cultivation for some time, quite a lot of hybridizing has been done, intentionally and unintentionally, and a good range of attractive flower colored forms are available.

It is slightly unfortunate that taxonomists pointed out in the early '90s that it is not possible to draw a good dividing line between the plants in *Echinopsis* and those in the genus *Trichocereus*. The latter have more or less identical flowers, but on the whole grow much larger and taller; they are therefore not quite so well suited to cultivation. Plants of *Trichocereus* may sometimes be encountered under the generic name *Echinopsis*, but cannot be expected to flower until considerably larger than plants in *Echinopsis*.

Long-cultivated species, such as *Echinopsis eyriesii*, *E. tubiflora*, *E. multiplex*, and *E. oxygona*, are probably rare as pure species but many plants derived from them are in cultivation and are worth growing. The flowers are mostly white or pink and can be as large as 8 in. (20cm) long and 6 in. (15cm) in diameter. It is a myth that

they will flower better if the offsets are removed. Given a good amount of root room, they will develop into large clumps and have many flowers. The yellow-flowered *E. aurea* is slightly less common but also makes a good clump; it is often one parent of some of the yellow-flowered hybrids.

Some of the slightly smaller *Echinopsis* were formerly included in the genus *Pseudolobivia*. They usually have smaller flowers, but make up for it by producing large numbers. If these plants are kept in a hot greenhouse they can lose large quantities of water when they produce a big crop of flowers; it helps to put them in a shaded position at this time. Typical species of this group are *E. ancistrophora* and *E. polyancistra*. Two

species with very striking colored flowers are *E. kermesina* (carmine-red) and *E. frankii* (deep pink).

Epiphyllum

These are commonly known as the orchid cacti. The species of the genus are relatively scarce in cultivation and do not do particularly well in a normal cactus greenhouse. In the wild they mostly grow epiphytically alongside orchids and bromeliads and need similar conditions. However, there has been more intentional hybridizing in this group than within any other group of cacti. This has not only produced a very wide variety of plants with spectacular flowers, but also has bred in greater hybrid vigor and tolerance of a

wider range of conditions. Thus, many of the hybrids make good indoor plants providing they are grown in reasonable light.

It must be understood that the epiphyllums need different conditions from the very xerophytic globular cacti. They require a richer soil with more humus in it and a feed with a rather higher percentage of nitrogen. While the hybrids are more resistant to cold than the species they still appreciate a bit more winter warmth than most cacti. The hybrid epiphyllums may have flowers up to 10 in. (25.5cm) in diameter and almost all flower colors (except blue) have been developed. Some that have *E. cooperi* in their parentage also have a strong perfume.

Surprisingly, epiphyllums are not often seen in garden centers, perhaps because their flowering season is rather short and the plants are not particularly attractive when not in flower. To find a good range of species go to a nursery that specializes in epiphylums, of which there are one or two in most large countries.

Above: Stunning flower of a large hybrid *Epiphyllum*.

Below: A delicately hued hybrid *Ephiphyllum*.

Espostoa

These plants originate in the Peruvian Andes, and make very attractive specimens. Most species are covered with a dense white wool and, although eventually they get quite large, they are not fast growing, so are quite popular in cultivation. In habitat they grow in very rocky soil on the sides of fairly steep valleys, but they are quite accommodating and seem to grow well in any well-drained soil. They are fairly tolerant of cold conditions but should be kept frost free for safety.

Like many plants of the Andes, each valley has its own population, which differs slightly from adjacent valleys and has been given a different species name, although the differences are rather marginal. *Espostoa lanata* is the oldest name for the larger-growing species which will eventually reach 8–9 ft. (2.5–2.75m) in height with fairly strong spines as well as the wool. *E. melanostele* rarely exceeds 3 ft. (1m) in height and has more fluffy dense white wool, and most forms are not so strongly spined.

When espostoas reach flowering size they produce a modified area in a groove on the side of the stem at the top. The areoles in this area produce copious wool and bristles and will eventually flower; this structure is called a cephalium. The plants need to be a fair age to get to this stage and conditions must be ideal, so flowering plants are not often seen in cultivation. It is believed that one of the factors that delays the production of the cephalium in cultivation is the unequal summer/winter daylight length in more northerly latitudes.

The plants formerly included in Thrixanthocereus are now generally included in this genus. They come from slightly further north in Peru and are not quite so tolerant of cold temperatures but are otherwise fairly easy to grow. They form their bristly cephaliums at slightly smaller sizes than the previous species. *E. senilis* has pure white spines, while *E. blossfeldiorum* have gray and black ones.

Espostoa melanostele exhibiting its fluffy, dense white wool. In its natural habitat this protects it from extremes of temperature.

Ferocactus

This group of attractive spiny barrel cacti are from Mexico and the United States. Some grow to quite large sizes and do not flower very easily in cultivation. However, they do make imposing specimens and are therefore quite popular. They are also easy to grow from seed, which is produced in large quantities resulting in them being seen frequently in garden centers.

Most species do best in a compost without too much humus and benefit from being given a fair amount of root room so that they can grow to maturity. One particular problem that can occur with some ferocactus arises from the fact that they have a gland on the areole that secretes a sugary substance. Under damp conditions this encourages the growth of the mold *Aspergillus niger*, which does not damage the plant but can be very unsightly. It can be brushed away with a small brush, but this is time consuming and exacting. Spraying with water at the right time to remove the nectar can work. In our greenhouses the nectar is often collected by ants, which certainly minimizes the problem. In drier climates this is unlikely to be a problem.

A few species do not normally grow quite so large and these would be best for the beginner. *Ferocactus (Hamatocactus) setispinus* is a small, very free-flowering species that does well on a window sill or in the greenhouse. The flowers are yellow with a red center, and the plant carries on flowering throughout the summer. The remaining species are probably more suited to greenhouse than indoor cultivation. *F. macrodiscus* is also small. It forms a broad flat head rarely more than 6 in. (15.25cm)

diameter, but grows into large clumps of several hundred heads. In our experience this species is somewhat reluctant to flower in cultivation.

F. stainesii is one of the larger-growing and most striking species of Ferocactus. Huge red-spined specimens with main stems 8 ft. (2.5m) tall and 2 ft. (60cm) in diameter and a dozen or so slightly smaller offsets can be found in the wild. It has attractive rings of orange-red flowers on the crown. In cultivation we have found it to be fairly slow; our largest plant has not reached flowering size although it must be a fair age.

Also quite large, although it usually remains solitary, is *F. wislizenii*. This grows in the same habitat as the carnegiea and needs the same very sunny, hot conditions. It has strong hooked spines and yellow flowers. Also from Arizona but spreading into California is *F. acanthodes* with long twisting red spines.

in diameter. It will produce attractive striped flowers at half this size. Slightly larger is *F. latispinus,* which will grow up to 12 in. (30.5cm) across and has characteristic broad, flattened spines. This species needs very good light to fully develop its characteristics. There are forms with red spines and

purple flowers and yellow spines and yellow flowers. Of similar size is *F. viridescens,* which grows near the coast in Southern California and adjacent peninsula Baja California. The name refers to the yellowish-green flowers.

F. glaucescens can be found growing alongside *Cephalocerus senilis* and *Astrophytum ornatum* in the Barranca de Metitzlan. As the name suggests, it has a

Ferocactus chrysacanthus is one the smaller-growing species and has a dense covering of fierce golden spines.

slightly glaucous stem, which can grow to around 1 ft. (30cm) in diameter. This species will offset to form small clumps of up to six to eight heads. The spines are yellow, as are the flowers. It needs to be around ten years old before it will flower. *F. robustus* has quite small heads only growing to 6 in. (15.25cm) or so in

Gymnocalycium

The gymocalyciums originate in South America, covering quite a wide area including Argentina, Paraguay, Uruguay, and adjacent areas of Bolivia. They are very easy to grow and flower, since they are tolerant of a wide range of conditions. The genus can be recognized by the appearance of the flower buds which are scaly.

G. bruchii comes in a wide variety of forms but is characterized by fairly small heads that proliferate into quite large clumps. Even very small plants will bear pale pink to whitish flowers. *G. baldianum* is very common and popular. It also flowers very easily with red to purplish flowers, it does offset, but not quite so freely as *G. bruchii*. *G. andreae* is similar with a clear yellow flower. *G. quehlianum* is a little

slower growing and tends to remain solitary. This species has silvery-white flowers. There are also some quite large-growing species in the genus such as *G. saglionis*. This one can make quite impressive specimens up to 18 in. (45cm) in diameter. The disadvantage is that it needs to be a little larger, around 4 in. (10cm) before it starts flowering. In spite of its name, *G. multiflorum* is not as free flowering as some species, but the flowers are larger than average for the genus.

G. mihanovichii is perhaps a little trickier to grow than some, preferring slightly warmer conditions, but it will also flower when quite small. There are a wide variety of forms of this species, some

Above: *Gymnocalycium mihanovicii* will flower when quite small but is tricky to grow.

Left: The large white flowers of *Gymnocalycium denudatum*.

of which have attractive purplish bodies. This species has also given rise to one of the oddities of the cactus world: when cacti are grown from seed, occasional mutant seedlings occur that lack chlorophyll. Normally these would perish, being unable to photosynthesize and manufacture food. However, in Japan some of these seedlings were grafted onto a green stock plant and preserved. Because they still contain the red pigment that shows as purple in the normal plant, these seedlings are bright red. They have been extensively propagated and are sometimes sold under the name "hibotan." They must always be grown grafted; indeed for optimum growth it is best to regraft periodically to retain the vigor. Variants of this plant with pink pigment or yellow plants

without the red pigment are now also on the market.

Also worth a place in any collection is *G. horridispinum*. Strongly spined, it grows slightly taller and forms occasional offsets. It produces lovely clear pink flowers. *G. gibbosum* is a widespread species with very stout spines and large white flowers. Some forms come from far south in Argentina, making them very cold tolerant. *G. denudatum* has stems with a rather small number of ribs and offsets to form small clumps; the flowers are white and large. *G. horstii*, a fairly recently discovered species, is quick growing and can make quite large clumps. The flowers range from pinkish to salmon in color.

Lobivia

The genus name is an anagram of Bolivia, their country of origin, although some of the species are found in adjacent areas of Peru. All grow at high altitudes. They adapt well to cultivation and are free flowering, the flowers being rather short-lived but diurnal as opposed to the related nocturnal-flowering echinopsis. They need good light conditions and prefer not to be too warm in winter, which can inhibit flowering.

Lobivia silvestrii (formerly named *Chamaecereus silvestrii*) is deservedly popular as it can put on massive displays of orange flowers and is exceedingly easy to propagate from cuttings. It needs plenty of food and water in the growing season, but it is essential to give it a cool, dry resting period to get it to flower well. It is one of those cacti that hybridizes freely. There are many hybrids with other lobivias in cultivation with a wide variety of flower colors. It also hybridizes with plants from a wide variety of other cactus genera.

Many of the lobivias such as *L. densispina* are extremely variable, particular in flower and spine color and a large number of different forms can be collected. The constant characteristic is that of very dense spination, which the name suggests.

Lobivias are very much affected by their growing conditions, for example those grown in poor light will have elongated stems and very poor spines compared to a plant grown in good light. *L. jajoiana* is also variable in having many flower colors. It tends to remain smaller than the previous species and rarely offsets. It is easily recognized when in flower as the base of the stamens are fused to form a dark collar at the base of the flower. *L. backebergii* has rather ordinary green stems but offsets into big clumps and is very easy to grow and flower; the flowers are red. *L. winteriana* is one of our favorite species; it tends to remain smaller, has few offsets and delicate pink flowers. *L. shieliana* has small shoots that multiply and form clumps of many heads, the spines are curly and in some forms white or cream. The flowers are brick red. With even

Lobivia jajoiana has many different flower colors. It rarely offsets and remains smaller.

smaller heads is *L. arachnacantha* with either red or yellow flowers. Its appearance is that of a miniature echinopsis.

This distinct group grows into giant plants. These are sometimes put into a separate genus, *Soehrensia*. They have close affinities with some species of *Trichocereus*. They can grow to several feet in diameter and height but will not flower until considerably larger than the other lobivias: typical is *L. bruchii*. A species with fine long spines is *L. formosa*. These plants need large pots or even free root run to attain their full potential.

Haageocereus

Haageocereus is a genus of columnar cacti originating in Peru. Many species have dense golden-yellow spines and are fairly easy to propagate from seed; thus, they are often propagated by the wholesale cacti nurseries. These plants need fairly sunny conditions to develop properly, so are not very suitable for indoor cultivation. Flowering is rare except in particularly good conditions or where the plants are given free root run. There are many slightly different forms with a variety of different names of which *H. versicolor* is perhaps the most frequently encountered. *H. decumbens* is a little different in that it has prostrate rather than erect stems; this one is a little easier to flower than the erect forms.

Hildewinteria

There is only one species in this genus, *Hildewinteria aureispina*. As the name suggests it has golden-yellow spines. This plant grows stems to 2–3 ft. (0.6–1 m) long and offsets freely to form fair-sized clumps. Because of its rather spreading, trailing habit, it can be a little difficult to accommodate. The best way to display it is in a normal pot placed on a pedestal above the level of the other plants. It is an extremely good species for flowers and probably has the longest flowering season of almost any cactus. We have had flowers on it from February to November.

Lophophora

This genus includes only a few species, but they are well known, if not notorious. The plant known as *Lophorphora williamsii* is also known as the peyote cactus. It contains a series of hallucinogenic alkaloids. The Native Americans knew this and used it in their religious ceremonies. The effects of these alkaloids have been studied in detail both by scientists and amateur experimenters who describe vivid multicolored hallucinations. Unfortunately for the experimenters, the cacti also contain alkaloids that have a strong emetic effect, so the results of eating the cactus are frequently unpleasant. Limited information suggests that in cultivation, at least in Europe, plants do not produce as high concentrations of the alkaloids as they do in habitat. In the United States and a few other countries, growing and possessing these plants is illegal because of their potential for misuse. Find out what your local laws are before growing them. Generally, in Europe, the plant is widely grown and does not cause any difficulties.

L.williamsii is an easy plant to grow and flower, and some forms make very pretty plants. It grows over a quite wide area of northern Mexico and is also found in southern Texas. There is quite a range of different forms, all spineless. The larger-headed forms are slower to form clumps; they often have slightly bluish bodies and tufted yellow wool in the areoles. The more rapidly proliferating forms seem somewhat more reluctant to flower. The flower color varies from a very pale pink to a deep purplish-pink.

Mammillaria

The genus Mammillaria is one of the largest genera of cacti and certainly one of the most popular. There are probably around 300 species occurring mostly in Mexico and the United States but with a few species from the West Indies and the northern coast of South America. Because of its popularity two specialty societies are well established, publishing quarterly journals in English and German.

Many mammillarias make ideal beginner's plants as they grow quickly and easily from seed and will flower when they are quite young. Although they often only have small flowers, they frequently make up for it by producing them in large numbers. Many species offset freely

Above: *Mammillaria hahniana* is a slow-growing clumping plant with long white hair.

Below: *Mammillaria deherdtiana* is another recently discovered miniature.

and can produce quite large spectacular clumps. Mammillarias are tolerant of a wide range of soils except for just a few tricky species that are slower growing and may need a slightly more sandy mix.

Perhaps the most commonly seen species is *M. zeilmanniana* with rings of deep pink flowers and short hooked spines. It offsets to produce quite big clumps. Although easy as small plants, larger clumps can be a bit more touchy and slightly more careful watering is advised. There is a white-flowered form as well, but this lacks some of the character of its more common cousin.

M. bocasana is a similar type of mammillaria, but this one is covered in white wool and has white to slightly pinkish flowers. It can get into sizable clumps in cultivation. M.bombycina can grow even larger, eventually reaching several feet in diameter with many hundreds of heads. The spines are longer and there are different forms with both yellow and brown spines. The flowers are pinkish. M.camptotricha can also grow into quite large clumps with long tubercles and long twisted spines. The flowers are small and white and have a distinct perfume.

Some species of mammillaria are very variable. In M. elongata, the constant feature is the elongated stem, but there are literally dozens of forms all with different spine colors and arrangements and different stem sizes. All can make fair sized clumps and have smallish white to cream flowers. Smaller again but very common is M. gracilis because the shoots are very weakly attached and readily fall off and root. Flowers and central spines are not produced until the central head reaches a reasonable size.

M. geminispina also makes large splendid specimens with strong white spines and is very easy to grow but rather more reluctant to flower until quite large. Some mammillarias have quite large, showy flowers. *M. longimamma*, although the plant is perhaps not so attractive as some, has yellow flowers up to 2 in. (5cm) in diameter. In *M. surculosa* the flowers are a little smaller, but also have a citrus smell. It makes a mass of small heads that spread across the soil, and big clumps can produce many flowers.

M. candida is an attractive white-spined plant that occasionally offsets. It likes a good sunny position. *M. elegans* can be quite slow growing and has tiny red flowers. At the other end of the scale, *M. guelzowiana*, although superficially like *M.*

bocasana, has very large flowers of an intense pinky-red. It is distinctly more difficult and should be in a well-drained compost and watered with care.

M. matudae is very free flowering and can make a good plant, although the heads sometimes become rather long and pendant, making the plant difficult to accommodate. Various forms of *M. woodsii* are frequently seen. This can make quite large single heads, although it will occasionally offset. The amount of wool is variable, but the flowers are always small and pink. *M. plumosa* is a popular species because of its feathery spines. It has an unusual habit of flowering in the winter, but does not

Above: *Mammillaria elegans.*

Below left: *Mammillaria nazacensis* is a recently discovered miniature mammillaria and benefits from a fairly sandy compost.

do so in cultivation unless a reasonable amount of winter sunshine is available.

Various forms of *M. rhodantha* are common in cultivation, this, like *M. elongata*, comes in a wide range of spine colors. As with a few other mammillarias, this species sometimes undergoes a splitting of the growing point into two or more growing points. This is termed "dichotomous branching." Another plant which does this is *M. parkinsonii*; it has dense white spines. *M. spinosissima* is yet another excellent flowering plant, frequently having several rings of flowers open together. Of a rather different type is *M. heyderi*, which forms usually solitary broad flat heads.

There are many species of more choice dwarf mammillaria to delight the specialist collector, such as *M.herrerae* with dense interlacing white spines on a body often not much more than 1 in. (2.5cm) in diameter and quite large pink flowers.

Most of the mammillarias are worth growing and a good collection will provide interest and flowers for much of the year.

Matucana

The matucanas are Peruvian plants, many growing at quite high altitudes, thus needing very good light. They have attractive spines and are well worth growing. Some species will offset, forming small clumps. *M. haynei* is perhaps the most common species in cultivation. It is quite variable, having forms with slightly different spine and flower colors ranging from carmine to scarlet. The flowers are about 2 in. (5cm) long and zygomorphic in shape. *M. aureiflora* has large somewhat flattened heads, is less spiny, and is atypical in having regular yellow flowers. A group of less spiny matucanas, including *M. paucicostata* and *M. madisoniorum*, grow at lower altitudes.

Melocactus

These plants are found in a number of countries. All need higher than average minimum winter temperatures to survive, as they come from relatively warm areas. A number of species come from the West Indies. Some are found in southern Mexico, and also the north coast of South America. Another group is found in the coastal valleys of Peru. There are also a considerable number of Brazilian species. The characteristic of the genus is the terminal cephalium from which the flowers and fruits are produced.

All the species are globular or short and cylindrical. When the plants become mature, the areoles at the apex of the plants modify to form a large amount of wool and frequently reddish bristles. No new photosynthetic plant tissue is produced, but the cephalium can continue to grow for many years. The small, pink flowers pop out of the cephalium in the afternoon. The pink fruits follow some months later. Most species appear to be self-fertile and large quantities of flowers, fruits and seed are produced by mature plants. The size of

the plants varies quite considerably from species to species and the larger-growing species naturally take longer to reach maturity. Younger plants seem more resistant to lower temperatures than mature plants with cephalia.

Probably the easiest species are the Brazilian ones. Plants such as *M. concinnus* and *M. bahiensis* can be grown from seed to flowering size in eight to ten years. Melocacti tend to have wide-spreading roots and appreciate growing in pans. They are also not very tolerant of alkaline soil, so it is important not to allow alkaline deposits to build up in the soil. Do not give melocacti too long a winter rest; some water in winter is definitely beneficial. *M. azureus*, a Brazilian species with a beautiful blue body, seems to be a little more difficult than *M. bahiensis* and must be kept reasonably warm.

The melocacti from the coastal areas of Venezuela and Mexico and the West Indies are mostly larger growing than the Brazilian species, making very handsome spiny specimens if kept sufficiently warm. The one exception is *M. matanzanus* from Cuba, which is perhaps the smallest melocactus, forming a cephalium when around six years old and 3 in. (7.5cm) in diameter. The cephalium's dense red bristles make it very striking.

The melocacti from Peru are perhaps the least cultivated and most difficult of the genus. They grow in very arid areas and are

Neoporteria villosa displaying its small pink flowers and bird's nest appearance.

sensitive to excess moisture. Some such as *M. belavistensis* are very attractive plants. All of the melocacti appreciate as much sun as possible.

Neobuxbaumia

This small group of Mexican cerei was formerly included in *Cephalocereus*, but these plants do not produce a cephalium before flowering. They get quite large and need plenty of room. All are night-flowering, and once they reach flowering size, possible in cultivation, they produce quite large numbers of flowers.

The quickest-growing and easiest species is *N. euphorbioides* from northern Mexico. It can grow 6–8 in. (15–20cm) a year and will start flowering at around 4–5 ft. (1.25–1.5m). The flowers are pale pink and 2 in. (5cm) across. It grows better if kept at more than 41°F (5°C).

N. polylopha comes from central Mexico and is rather slow growing, at least in its younger stages. The stem is a good deal thicker and has many more ribs and, for us, only grows at 2–3 in. (5–7.5 cm) a year. Our plant, which is around 4 ft. (1.25m) tall started flowering in 1996. The flowers are smaller than *N. euphorbioides* and a deeper red. We find this species marks fairly easily unless kept warmer, say around 50°F

(10°C). It is therefore quite surprising that large specimens of this species are grown outside in the exotic gardens in Monaco and other places on the French Riviera. It can eventually grow to more than 20 ft. (6m). Other species such as *N. tetetzo* appear not to take well to cultivation.

Neoporteria

A group of mostly small plants coming from Chile with a few species in Argentina and Peru. They take well to greenhouse cultivation and will flower at small sizes. They do need good light and are probably unlikely to flower in indoor cultivation. Many come from quite arid areas and need a well-drained mineral compost and careful watering, particularly species with large tap-roots. The taxonomists have been busy in this group, so you may also find the plants under the generic names of *Neochilenia*, *Pyrrhocactus*, and *Horridocactus*.

The plants of the *Neochilenia* group are the smallest and mostly have large tap roots. They can be very free flowering, even as quite young plants. The flowers are usually rather subtle colors, pale pinks

Notocactus

This very popular group of cacti occurs in Uruguay, Paraguay, Argentina, and southern Brazil. For the most part easy to grow and flower, they make good indoor plants. They prefer an acid peat-based compost and should not be given too long a dry rest period. Many species are worth growing, and quite a wide range of forms and flower colors is available. *N. ottonis* is a very common species occuring over quite a wide area, consequently there are a number of different forms. It forms underground stolons and eventually produces clumps of quite a few heads. The flowers are a clear yellow, appear in the spring and are 2–3 in. (5–7.5cm) in diameter. *N. mammulosus* is also a very easy plant to grow. It has stouter, sharper, and slightly flattened spines compared to *N. ottonis*. The flowers are yellow and bell-shaped. *N. concinnus* tends to remain solitary and has long curly spines. The flowers are large— up to 4 in. (10cm) in diameter—and very freely produced. The more recently discovered *N. uebelmannianus* also usually remains solitary. The flowers are smaller, but in one form they can be a pink to purple color.

A group of larger plants is sometimes placed into a separate genus, Eriocactus. *N. leninghausii* is a deservedly popular species very commonly seen in cultivation. With golden spines and many ribs, it grows into a short columnar plant that branches

and creams are common, and about 2 in. (5cm) in diameter. Often the body colors are also interesting with shades of purple and brown pigments. They slowly offset to form small clumps. Typical species are *N. napina* and *N. esmeraldana*. There are some slightly larger, more spiny species in this group, such as *N. paucicostata*.

Plants belonging to the genus Neoporteria in the narrower sense usually have very dense, bird's-nest-like spines. Their smallish pink flowers have a characteristic partially opened appearance and paler centers. On some species the flowers unusually appear in the autumn/winter. Due to their spines, they make very attractive plants. With age they become quite a bit taller than wide. Typical are *N. villosa*, *N. wagenknecktii*, and *N. nidus*.

A further group of stoutly spined plants have been placed in *Horridocactus*. They have unusual coppery- or greenish-colored flowers. On the whole they need to be slightly larger to flower than the other species. Typical of this group is *N. tubersiculata*.

***Notocactus leninghausia* is a popular, commonly cultivated species.**

from the base to form clumps. This plant must be a little larger than other notocacti before it flowers; the flowers are usually produced in big bunches from the tops of the stems, are relatively long lasting and, unusually, stay open at night. *N. leninghausii*, like a few other plants from this group, has a tendency to grow with the top on a slant. This is quite natural. *N. magnificus*, a recently described species related to *N. leninghausii*, has shorter broader stems with fewer deeper ribs and a bluish color to the body. It also grows into quite large clumps and can make magnificent

specimens.

At the other end of the scale is *N. rutilans,* which rarely exceeds 3 in. (7.5cm) in height and 2 in. (5cm) in diameter. It flowers when quite small; the pink flowers shade into yellow at the center. *N. scopa* is another common species that comes in a wide variety of spine colors. Most forms are solitary and usually have yellow flowers. A very different type of plant is *N. haselbergii*; this is globular with dense glassy white spines and long-lasting red flowers. The similar yellow-spined *N. graessneri* has green flowers.

Opuntia

This is the largest genus of cacti and most widely dispersed, having some 300 species growing from Canada to Patagonia and from the West Indies to the Galapagos Islands.

The genus is diverse and various attempts have been made to split it into smaller genera. Opuntias, particularly the prickly pears, have become widely naturalized in many areas and in some places have become a serious weed.

All the opuntias contain in their areoles small spines called glochids. These have minute barbs and they very easily become detached and embedded in the skin and can be very irritating, so care must be taken in handling these plants. Some species also have a barbed sheath over the spines, which can also be very painful. These factors tend to make this group of plants unpopular, a pity because there are some very interesting forms and many have very beautiful flowers. Some species become quite large, so, unless space is not a problem, concentrate on the smaller, slower-growing species.

The flat-padded opuntias are the most familiar, and perhaps one of the most common in cultivation is O. microdasys. This Mexican species has dense glochids but no spines. In the typical form the glochids are brown and the pads 2–3 in. (5–7.5cm) in diameter. The flowers are yellow.

Many opuntias are cultivated for the fruit, which can either be eaten directly or turned into jams or preserves. For this purpose various strains of relatively spineless opuntias have been developed. Some of these derive from

Above:
Opuntia vestita is in a group of cylindrical species from South America.

Below left: *Opuntia ficus-indica* in cultivation showing the size to which it will grow.

O. ficus-indica. On the whole these are too large and uninteresting for horticultural purposes.

A number of more attractive species come from the southern United States. These include O. violacea with purplish pads, long black spines, and yellow flowers with a red center. Fairly similar is O. chlorotica, which grows somewhat larger and has slightly bluer pads. O. basilaris, a very desirable species, grows in California and Arizona. It makes small clumps of pads that stay close to the ground. The pads are somewhat bluish and the flower is a lovely cerise pink. Do not keep it too warm in the winter or it will not flower. In dry conditions it should be fairly hardy. Another plant with a similar habit is O. erinacea; this has a dense covering of long white spines and has varieties with pink or yellow flowers. This one will withstand even colder conditions. Some opuntias grow very far north in the United States, such as O. polyacantha. They are mostly very low-growing plants that stay close to the ground and are very hardy even in the most extreme conditions.

Mexico has many species of flat-padded opuntias including perhaps one of the largest padded species, O. robusta. This can make pads some 18 in. (45cm) in diameter and can get to be a very large plant, so it is only suitable for cultivation if you have plenty of space and can perhaps give it a free root run. The pads are also a nice glaucous blue color. O. stenopetala is also an interesting species that produces a lateral series of pads running across the ground, rooting as they go. It has small red to orange flowers produced in large numbers. Other Mexican species commonly seen in cultivation include O. pailana, which is very spiny

and gets quite tall, and *O. scheeri*, which has wispy spines that also occur on the flower buds and fruit. Another popular species is *O. pycnantha* from Baja California. This one is relatively slow growing and needs more cautious watering. Its flowers are relatively small and yellow.

Flat-padded opuntias are not confined to North and Central America. A very interesting large-growing species occurs on the Galapagos Islands. *O. galapageia* grows a massive spiny trunk and a big canopy of branches. *O. brasiliensis* also grows a large woody central trunk and has small very thin laterals, which are shed after a few years. This species has small yellow flowers. A further interesting group of small flat-padded opuntias come from Argentina.

These have pads no more than 2 in. (5cm) long and spread sideways across the ground. They flower quite easily and most, such as *O. erectoclada*, have quite large red flowers.

A very different group of opuntias are the chollas, which grow in northern Mexico and the southern United States. These plants have rather woody cylindrical stems that are very spiny and do not grow very well in cultivation unless with very sunny conditions and given a lot of space. Such plants as *O. bigelowii* and *O. tunicata* may look very attractive from a distance, but it not advisable to get too close to them. There is a group of lower-growing opuntias with small club-shaped stems. Some of them are worth growing because they have interesting spines and some will

flower when not too large. *O. invicta* has very strong spines, usually red when young. It is the largest of this group but relatively slow growing. The smallest, *O. planibulbispina*, has joints less than 1 in. (2.5cm) in length and small dagger-like white spines.

The cylindrical opuntias from South America are rather different. Some of the species, such as *O. subulata*, have large leaves and can be very rampant in growth. But the group also contains some choice slower-growing species, such as *O. pachypus*, which will not grow more than 2–3 in. (5–7.5cm) a year. The group also contains one or two fairly low-growing, high-altitude

plants that are relatively hardy, such as *O. verschaffeldtii*, with pleasing red flowers, and *O. vestita* with its dense covering of wide hairs. *O. salmiana* is perhaps the easiest of opuntias to flower, the thin stems producing many flowers and seed pods. It falls to pieces at the slightest touch, each joint rooting and forming new plants.

A number of South American opuntias are sometimes put in the genus *Tephrocactus*. They have globular joints and are relatively slow growing. Mostly high-altitude plants, they need very good light and can be somewhat reluctant to flower.

Pachycereus

Another genus of cerei, Pachycereus, includes some of the largest-growing cacti. The most commonly seen is *P. pringlei*, which comes from Baja California and adjacent areas on the mainland of Mexico. Seedlings are produced in large numbers by the wholesale cacti growers, and it is commonly seen on sale in garden centers. It is quite easy to grow and makes quite a handsome pot plant.

For optimum growth it requires a large pot or free root run and good sunny conditions. This plant can eventually reach nearly 40 ft. (12m) in height, but such plants are very old. Other species of *Pachycereus* such as *P. weberi* come from somewhat farther south in Mexico and are a bit fussier about being kept warm. *P. weberi* is a contender for the title of "largest cactus" because, although it might not grow quite so tall, it forms a massive candelabra of branches.

Parodia

This group of South American cacti is from Argentina and Bolivia. They are globular, short, cylindrical, and produce good displays of flowers when quite small. Their roots are often a little on the weak side, so it is important not to let the soil become too alkaline with a build-up of salts. Many of the species have hooked spines, but there are exceptions such as the popular golden-spined *P. chrysacanthion* with yellow flowers. The hooked-spined species may have yellow (*P. aureispina*) or red (*P. sanguiniflora*) flowers. There are many larger-growing species with long hooked spines such as *P. maassii*. These have comparatively small flowers. A few species such as *P. marnieriana* will offset to form clumps, this has rather small orange-red flowers. Many species such as *P. schwebsiana* produce much white wool from the new growth.

Above: This cholla opuntia is really too dangerous to have in an average collection.

Below: *Parodia chrysacanthion*, which has ring after ring of golden yellow flowers.

Oreocereus

Oreocereus are frequently seen in cultivation because of their attractive long white hairs. They come from high parts of the Andes in Peru and Bolivia and appreciate very good light. Known as the old man of the Andes, these plants can eventually reach 4 ft. (1.25m) or so in height and have a few dozen stems, but they are quite slow growing and such plants must be many years old. However, they are very tough plants and not difficult to grow. Do not expect flowers in cultivation unless conditions are exceptionally good.

Most common is *O. celsianus*, which develops long hairs and very sharp spines. Even slower and more densely woolly is *O. trollii*. There are some less attractive, faster-growing species with less wool, such as *O. fossulatus*. They are a little more inclined to flower in cultivation. The flowers vary from pink to a reddish-brown and are zygomorphic, like those of the matucanas.

Pilosocereus

The genus *Pilosocereus* is a widespread group of columnar cacti, formerly included in the genus Cephalocereus. They come from Mexico, the West Indies, northern South America, while the largest number of species are found in Brazil.

Although relatively large-growing plants, they are commonly cultivated because they have attractive colored stems. The wholesale cacti nurseries grow large numbers of pilosocereus because they are easy to grow from seed and make eye-catching plants.

P. palmeri is the species that has been in common cultivation for many years. It originates in Mexico. Although it eventually reaches around 15 ft. (4.5m) in height, it starts flowering at a manageable 3–4 ft. (1–1.25m). The stem color varies from green to a slaty blue color in some forms. The flower is nocturnal, pink, and about 3 in. (7.5cm) in diameter. The areoles have a small amount of wool except for those bearing the flowers, which have a much denser woolly covering—a characteristic of the genus. There are a number of other species from Mexico, but the names reflect a certain amount of confusion.

One other that can be easily identified is *P. chrysacanthus* with its

covering of golden yellow spines. They will grow quite quickly given generous-sized pots or free root run.

A number of species come from the West Indies. They are quite fast growing and will make attractive plants, but they do need more heat than the Mexican species. Both *P. nobilis* and *P. barbadensis* are seen from time to time.

The Venezuelan species also need very warm conditions, but there are some very attractive plants including the recently described *P. tillianus* with long fine golden spines.

The Brazilian species used to be rather rare in cultivation, but are now grown in huge numbers for the wholesale market. Some species have bright blue stems, the color caused by a waxy covering on the epidermis. This persists for quite a few years, but eventually wears off with age. Although these plants do appreciate greater warmth than most cacti, they are not as fussy as the West Indian species and are quite robust and easy to grow. They are fast growing and many flower at a surprisingly small size, perhaps around 2 ft. (60cm) in height. The flowers are white, nocturnal, and have a somewhat unpleasant sickly smell that attracts the bats and moths that pollinate them in the wild. The fruits are quite large and have deep

Pilocereus glaucescens, from Brazil, showing the beginnings of a lovely blue stem.

red flesh. When these split open the contrast of the red flesh against the blue stem color is intense.

Recommended species include *P. pentaedrophorus* with relatively thin five-angled blue stems and small flowers, *P. magnificus* with thicker intense blue stems with more ribs, *P. fulvilanatus* with five-angled thick stems and long golden hairs in the flowering areoles, and *P. chrysostele* with more ribs and dense golden-yellow spines.

Rebutia

The genus *Rebutia* contains ideal speciesfor the novice cactophile. They are very easy to grow and many species will flower by the time they are two years old in conditions no more demanding than a sunny window sill. They flower in the spring, from around the base of the plants, and there is a good range of flower colors from reds to pinks to yellows. Some species can grow into quite large clumps and produce many hundreds of flowers each year. Some of the species have become hybridized as they readily set seed in cultivation. The commoner species include *R. senilis* with white spines

and usually red flowers, *R. marsoneri* with yellow flowers, and *R. minuscula* with red to pink flowers.

Easily recognizable are *R. fiebrigii* with rather longer spines and orange flowers, and *R. krainziana* with red flowers and very short, white spines. *R. heliosa*, a relatively recent discovery, is smaller with very tight pectinate spines. It is a little more difficult than *R. krainziana* and should be watered rather more sparingly or put in a slightly more porous compost. We also find *R. muscula* a little more difficult than the average rebutia; this species has dense white spines and orange flowers. Another relatively new species is *R. perplexa*, which has fairly small heads and pale pink flowers.

From a slightly different group of rebutias we have *R. pygmaea*. This is a little slower growing, has salmon-pink flowers, and is very prone to attack by red spider mite.

Rhipsalis

This group of epiphytic cacti, mainly from Brazil, likes the same conditions as orchids and bromeliads. The soil should be acidic and peat based and the plants should not be given prolonged dry spells. Frequent mist spraying of the stems is beneficial. Under these conditions they are easy to grow and make ideal hanging-basket plants. They are very suitable for indoor cultivation, but regrettably only seem to be available through specialty nurseries. The flowers are small and mostly white, but borne in great profusion, sometimes several from each areole, an unusual feature for cacti. There are quite a large number of species varying greatly in stem shape from broad flattened stems to thin cylindrical ones.

Commonly grown species include *R. mesembryanthoides* with thin cylindrical stems, *R. pentaptera* with thicker five-angled winged stems, *R. crispimarginata* with broad flat wavy stems, and *R. houletiana* with thin, flat, slightly bluish stems.

Schlumbergia

This genus includes the well-known Christmas cactus. This is not actually a species but a hybrid of horticultural origin. Most plants now sold as Christmas cacti have a slightly different parentage and also have a wider range of flower colors. The newer forms often flower slightly earlier in the year prior to Christmas; the older hybrids more often than not did not actually flower at Christmas, but

A display of mixed *Schlumbergia* (Christmas cacti).

A young stenocactus exhibiting the characteristic wavy multiribbing.

more frequently in January or February. The flowering of Christmas cacti is triggered by the shortening day length and it is important not to disrupt this with too much artificial light. Like the rhipsalis, they are "jungle" cacti and need acidic peat-based soils, no long dry periods, and regular misting to create a humid atmosphere. The plants can eventually become quite large and put on very impressive flowering displays with hundreds of blooms at once. The traditional Christmas cactus has magenta-pink flowers, but newer forms have many variations. There is a pure white one which, however, will show traces of pink in the flowers unless kept fairly warm.

There are also some related species that flower slightly later in the year. *S. gaetneri*, called the Easter cactus, has smaller scarlet flowers. Christmas cacti are sometimes grafted on a tall, strong-growing cereus to produce a "standard." This can produce a very spectacular specimen.

Stenocactus

This group, also known as *Echinofossulocactus*, comes from northern Mexico. They are characterized by globular bodies with large numbers of wavy ribs, mostly flattened spines, and small striped flowers. They are somewhat related to the ferocacti but mostly stay much smaller.

The species are rather variable and somewhat difficult to distinguish. *S. albatus* has small yellowish flowers and yellow to white spines. *S. crispatus* has longer spines and pink-striped flowers. *S. coptonogonus* is unusual in having a small number of straight ribs.

Stenocereus

From Mexico and the United States comes a group of large treelike cacti. Because they are easy to grow from seed and have attractively marked stems as young seedlings, they are popular with the wholesale cacti growers. To grow them to mature sizes, however, requires rather a lot of space and also quite warm conditions for some species.

S. thurberi, the organ-pipe cactus, is the only species that crosses the border into the United States. With brownish felted areoles, it has an appeal, but it is not too easy to grow in cultivation; like the carnegiea that grows with it, it needs very hot sunny conditions. This plant can eventually reach 20 ft. (6m) in height.

S. pruinosus and S. chichipe come from further south in Mexico and, although faster growing, they may object to too cold conditions in winter. The chalky markings on their stems, prominent as seedlings, are not quite as pronounced in mature plants.

S. beneckei is perhaps the species most suitable for cultivation: it is smaller and shrubbier and the stems have a dense coating of white meal. Unfortunately, it is very sensitive to winter cold. The very odd cactus known as the creeping devil, which originates in the Baja California peninsula, is also usually placed here under modern classification. Its scientific name is S. eruca and it grows with the stems lying down on the ground, rooting into the sand as it grows. Eventually the older parts of the stem dry up, hence the epithet "creeping." It can be grown in cultivation, but its habit makes it awkward for pot cultivation; an open bed is more suitable.

Thelocactus lloydii, a small, globular cacti from Bolivia. It prefers a clay half-pot and a high mineral content in the soil, and will reward you with shining, deep pink and red flowers.

Sulcorebutia

The sulcorebutias are high-altitude plants from Bolivia. They are relatively small and globular, forming small clumps. These plants are free flowering in cultivation when given good light and are not particularly difficult to grow. There is a bewildering variety of intense flower colors, including even some bicolored forms. A common characteristic is elongated rather than circular areole.

All the species are worth growing and among those most commonly seen are S. candiae, one of the larger-growing species with golden spines and yellow flowers; S. steinbachii with red or pinkish flowers; S. glomeriseta with dense white spines and yellow flowers; S. canigueralii with bicolored flowers—orange with a yellow center; and S. arenacea with very neat symmetrical spination and yellow flowers.

Thelocactus

This group of very spiny, globular cacti comes from northern Mexico and the southern United States. Under good sunny conditions they produce large showy flowers. On the whole they prefer a well-drained, mineral-based compost. *T. bicolor* is a widespread species with a large number of forms all differing in size, shape, and spine color. All have pink flowers 3–4 in. (7.5–10cm) in diameter with a deeper red midstripe in the center and of a very glossy texture. They are fairly slow growing, perhaps needing less than average water. *T. hexaedrophorus* has a more open, flatter body and pure white flowers. There are some slightly larger-growing species such as *T. lophothele* which has prominently tubercled bodies and long spines. Their flowers are yellow to pale pink.

Thelocactus lloydii is a plant somewhat allied to *T. bicolor;* it has a similar flower but has a much more open flattened body and very strong spines.

Trichocereus

This is a group of large columnar cacti from Argentina, Chile, and Bolivia; at the smaller sizes it intergrades with the genus *Echinopsis.* They have similar large, mostly white, nocturnal flowers. They are very vigorous growing plants frequently used as stocks for grafting;

Trichocereus candicans showing the multitude of heads this species acquires with age. The heads on this plant are 6 in. (15cm) across and are up to 18 in. (45cm) long.

if adequate space is available they are well worth growing for their own merits.

Some of the lower-growing clumping varieties flower at the smallest sizes. Typical is *T. schickendantzii* with 10 in. (25.5cm) diameter pure white flowers. With even shorter,

thicker stems is *T. candicans,* which comes in a wide variety of forms.

The plants from Chile, *T. chilensis,* have very strong spines and are somewhat slower growing and more reluctant to flower. *T. macrogonus* is much taller growing with slightly blue stems. It needs to be around 6 ft. (1.8m) or more to flower but can reach this height very quickly under favorable conditions.

The real giants of the genus can get to 30 ft. (9m) or more and 2 ft. (0.60m) in diameter. They are slower growing but a good deal faster than their North American counterparts. *T. pasacana* and *T. terscheckii* fall in this group.

There are also some trichocereus with colored flowers that intergrade with the genus Lobivia. They are a good deal smaller and will flower at manageable sizes. *T. huascha* and *T. grandiflora,* usually with red flowers, belong to this group.

Turbinicarpus

This is a genus of rather rare miniature cacti from Mexico. They are quite slow growing but on the whole not particularly difficult if treated with care. Seedlings are readily available from specialty nurseries, and they start flowering at quite small sizes. As they develop into small clumps they are probably best grown in clay pots and a fairly mineral-based soil for safety. All species are worth growing with *T. lophophoroides* being a little more temperamental than most.

Uebelamannia

This unusual genus of just a few species is from the hot dry areas of northeast Brazil. These plants are difficult in cultivation and are frequently grown grafted. They have unusual gum cells in the epidermis, which make it glisten. The flowers are small and insignificant.

Succulents

Adenium
(Apocynaceae)

This increasingly popular genus of succulent plants comes from Africa and southern Arabia. The common names are desert rose, impala lily, mock azalea, desert azalea, and sabi star—for the simple reason that this plant has beautiful, showy flowers—and masses of them when the growing conditions are right.

Coming from these hot areas, it needs well-drained compost and extra heat in winter. This is a very good houseplant subject and looks good in a blue-and-white Chinese pot. The plants are usually multi-branched and in the wild can achieve heights of 10 ft. (3m), and have great swollen trunks, like great rocks sitting in the desert. They flower at a relatively young age depending on the conditions, possibly within two years from seed, but more usually about three to four years.

Most commonly available is *Adenium obesum*, from Tanzania and Natal. The five-petaled flowers are pink, but some varieties have white flowers. The horticultural trade is working on breeding plants with larger flowers, so watch out for this plant in the future.

Propagation is usually from seed, but cuttings may be taken to salvage a plant that is rotting.

Adromischus
(Crassulaceae)

Adromischus are attractive, small, low-growing, leafy succulents closely related to the genus *Cotyledon*. They are not in the least bit hardy away from their native South Africa and Namibia, but they can be grown outdoors in pots for the frost-free months of the year, slugs and snails willing. Many of the species have intense red/brown markings or patterns on their leaves, which are intensified by good light. Some species also have textured leaves, like *Andromischus marianae*; others have crinkled or wavy leaf edges, such as *A. cristatus*; yet others, like *A. leucophyllus* have a white coating to the leaves, a farina; this makes them less suitable for the open air, as this farina can be washed off in heavy rains.

Cultivation is simple, for they mostly grow quite readily from leaves set in a sandy soil mixture. No two plants seem to be exactly the same, for the markings are unique to each plant, unless they are produced from leaves from the same parent. The flowers are not really worth comment: a long stalk with small pink or white flowers set close to the stem. *A. grandiflora*, as the name suggests, has the largest flowers.

Aeonium
(Crassulaceae)

This relatively small genus of plants is from the Canary Islands, Cape Verde Islands, Madeira, and North Africa. They are often seen in garden centers, particularly the variety of plant with dark maroon leaves. Among these are *Aeonium arboreum* var. "Atropurpureum," or *A. arboreum* "Schwartzkopf," even darker and more vigorous; the latter are very useful for summer bedding, but need to be lifted, potted, and given protection before any frosts arrive.

The growth habit for these plants is a tall (often over 18 in./45cm) naked stem with a rosette of leaves on top, shiny or matte, occasionally hairy leaves (*A. smithii* and *A. simsii*), with a terminal inflorescence. Luckily, before it flowers the plant has usually had several side shoots, so all is not lost; additionally, the plant may set seed. The flowers are usually yellow, occasionally white or pink (*A.nobile*), and the inflorescence will have upward of a hundred small flowers arranged pyramidically, with the flowers opening in succession over a long period.

One species, *A. tabuliforme*, does not have shoots, but grows flush with the ground often attaining, in cultivation, the size of a dinner plate. Cultivation for this species is from seed or occasionally from leaves. *A cristate* or the monstrose form of this is more often available; by taking the small individual heads off this, normal plants can sometimes be grown.

Adromischus marrionae var. herreri.

Agave
(Agavaceae)

These highly architectural, rosette-forming, mostly stemless succulents are found naturally, predominantly on the North American continent and offshore islands. A sharp spine is at the tips of the leaves of most species, and also, in many species, there is a series of sharp teeth along the outer leaf margins, which are saw-like and can leave a nasty tear in the skin if handled roughly. The plants range in size from 6 in. (15cm) to 16 ft. (5m). Some of the species will tolerate quite cold conditions but will want extra drainage if planted in the open ground. It is beneficial to plant the rosettes at an angle, so that moisture does not collect in the center—the most tender part of the plant—and can drain away quickly.

The most commonly encountered species are *Agave americana* and its varieties, *A. american* "Variegata" (yellow stripe down the leaf margins) and *A. americana* "Medio-picta" (white stripe in the middle of the leaf, running from tip to base). The latter is usually the most expensive, being a little slower to make a large specimen. None of these three is totally hardy; the first two may survive some

Agave victoria-reginae from Nuevo Leon in Mexico makes large handsome specimens.

winters unharmed, but a bad winter will kill them if they are not protected from the elements in some way. *A. victoria-reginae* from Mexico, is a very handsome species with many white lines on the leaves; these lines are formed while the new leaves are compacted at the center of the plant and as the leaves unfold or open out so the white lines are left behind. *A. parviflora* does the same, but additionally has curling white filaments at the leaf edges.

Here is a very rough guide to which agaves are hardy: those with blue or fairly thin leaves are the most likely to be cold tolerant, while the fatter and paler green-leaved species are likely to come from a warmer environment.

The common name for these plants is century agave. This is somewhat of a misnomer, because the majority of species flower long before they are a hundred years old. However, they do have to "gather" themselves for the effort of flowering, and after they flower the rosette dies. Hopefully, during its lifetime the agave will have produced some offsets, or it will produce seed from which new plants may be grown. It is important to regularly repot the larger-growing species to enable them to attain their true potential, but this can be a hazardous experience. It can also be difficult to find a movable pot large enough.

Aichryson
(Crassulaceae)

Aichrysons are biennial plants for the most part. Closely related to aeoniums, they are very much smaller hairy-leaved cousins from the Canary Islands off the west coast of Africa. These yellow-flowered plants may be grown out of doors, but only in the most sheltered of parts in southern England.

They are summer flowering and do well if kept outdoors for the better months, then moved inside before a frost. They flower terminally but luckily are self fertile, producing masses of small seed that scatters everywhere, germinating like mustard and cress. Once this plant has been acquired, it is most unlikely to leave you.

Aloe
(Asphodelaceae)

Aloes belong to a very large family containing some 300 genera and 4,500 species. The genera which are closely related to Aloe and widely grown are *Bulbine, Bowiea, Ornithogalum* (the last two not considered succulents by some experts), *Haworthia, Astroloba, Lomatophyllum,* and *Gasteria*. The aloes are

Above: *Aloe pratensis* is a smaller-growing species from South Africa.

Below: Aichrysons are short-lived succulents that grow very easily from seed.

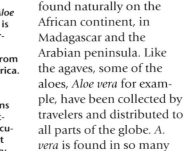

found naturally on the African continent, in Madagascar and the Arabian peninsula. Like the agaves, some of the aloes, *Aloe vera* for example, have been collected by travelers and distributed to all parts of the globe. *A. vera* is found in so many locations that its original habitat is not known.

These plants are often confused with agaves, and in part this must be due to the teeth that many of the aloes have, although these are usually much softer and do not normally cause damage. Like the agaves, they mostly grow in rosettes, but sometimes this characteristic is not that evident and it may only happen with age. Unlike agaves they should, once they start, flower annually; the flower is not terminal and will sometimes lead to the plant branching dichotomously. The flower spike often comes from a little way out of the center of the plant, it may be simple or branched. The flower colors range from white

through yellow and orange to red, some even have green flowers. Many of the aloes want to grow in the winter months in the northern hemisphere, which means that they will have to be given some water during the coldest months in the northern hemisphere.

Aloes come in a variety of sizes, ranging from 1 in. (2.5cm) to 58 ft. (18m) in height, and can have stems or trunks up to 10 ft. (3m), so it is important to select the right one for your conditions.

The most common species offered for sale is *A. aristata*. Do not discard this as not worth growing: It flowers most reliably and is very generous with its offsets, making it an ideal plant to propagate for fund-raising events.

A. *variegata* (partridge breast aloe) must be the second most commonly grown species of this genus; it seems to be particularly well suited to window sill cultivation and enjoys being pot-bound and baked by the sun. Because it will not be repotted regularly it needs to be watered and fed during the winter, otherwise it will not produce its very lovely flower spikes in the early spring. It offsets with

age and these can be removed and grown in separate pots. We have also grown this species outdoors all year round, but always in a very dry spot.

Two very statuesque aloes that may appear in your local garden center or nursery are A. *dichotoma* and A. *pillansii*. These are "tree" aloes; i.e, they have very thick trunks and can attain the height of small trees. A. *pillansii* is an endangered species in the wild with only a few specimens left and no regeneration. This sorry plight has probably been caused by overgrazing and possibly collecting; however, other factors such as changing climate may be playing a

Right: *Aloe ericacea*, a very xero-phytic slow-growing species.

Below: The attractive leaf color of *Aloe gariepensis* in its natural habitat.

part. A. *dichotoma*, on the other hand, is very common in the wild and in many areas is the only "tree" to be seen. It is used by the sociable weaver birds to house their huge communal nests.

In cultivation this plant must be repotted regularly if it is to grow well; a deficiency in either food or water will result in the leaves dying back from the tips.

Opposite:
A large tree forming aloe (*Aloe alooides*) in its natural habitat. This species is not suitable for pot culture.

Left: *Aloe melanocantha* is an attractive slow-growing species.

Right: The very popular *Aloe variegata*.

Below: *Aloe striata* has one of the more attractive inflorescences in the genus.

A. plicatilis is another "tree" aloe; although this species does not attain the same proportions as the previous two, neither does it grow so rapidly. It will, on the other hand, flower at a much younger age even when grown in a pot. Winter growing and flowering in the northern hemisphere, this strap-leaf aloe branches both before and with flowering. It is one of the few aloes that does not form a rosette of leaves.

A. jucunda, from Somalia, is a small-headed, spotted aloe that clumps with age into a plant 2–3 ft. (60cm–1m) across if you wish. It offsets freely, so there is no problem keeping this plant to the proportions you can accommodate; the removed offsets can then be repotted and passed on to friends. This plant flowers freely and many times during the summer months in the northern hemisphere, only ceasing when the light levels drop too low. It is a very glossy-leaved species with fairly hard teeth along the leaf margins. Hybrids are available as it has been crossed with A. haworthioides, A. belatula, and A. rauhii, to name but three. Other aloes in this group that are equally worthwhile to grow are A. peckii, A. somaliensis, A. kingiana, A. mcloughlanii, and A. hemmingsii. Most are considerably larger.

A. erinacea, A. pachygaster, and A. melanacantha are all desirable species to grow, the latter reaching the largest proportions. A. melanacantha has leaves with a very rough surface, with strong, black teeth or spines along the leaf margins. These spines are pale yellow and soft when the leaves first emerge from the center of the plant, but they harden and darken as they mature. A. erinacea and A. pachygaster are Namibian species, whereas A. melanacantha occurs up the west coast of South Africa and just into Namibia. A. erinaceae and A. pachygaster have a beautiful blue appearance to the leaves and again the strong, dark spines.

Note: They do not take kindly to being overwatered and require full sun.

Aloinopsis
(Aizoaceae)

These little plants are to be found in Cape Province of South Africa. They are low growing, without stems aboveground but have a thickened or swollen stem or rootstock below ground. The leaves are light gray, gray-brown, or green; many species have tubercles but not all, and some appear toothed. The flowers are either yellow, yellow with a red mid-stripe, or pink.

Three of the species, *Aloinopsis rosulata*, *A. rubro-lineata*, and *A. schoonesii*, have a similar epidermis, reminiscent of a lizard's skin. *A. schooneesii* has an extremely large tuberous rootstock compared with the amount of growth above ground, as they say of an iceberg, 10 percent aboveground and 90 percent below ground.

The only species with a pink flower is *A. spathulata*, which are set off well against the grayish-pink, spathulate leaves. Extra drainage is recommended and they like to grow in late summer/autumn/winter. Propagation is from seed; although they can be rooted from cut-tings this is usually only done to rescue a plant that would otherwise die.

Other related genera requiring similar treatment are *Delianthe*, *Nananthus*, and *Rabiea* with *Titanopsis* (see page 118).

Ceropegiea
(Asclepiadaceae)

Ceropegiea is a large genus of 150 species approximately, which grow in the wild from Africa to the Far East. They are mostly vining, twining plants, although several species on the Canary Islands, (*Ceropegiea fusca*, *C. dichotoma*, *C. hians*) have taken succulence a degree further by developing fatter, jointed stems and not vining. A few species have evolved their method of water storage in the other direction by developing underground tubers.

With a few exceptions these are fairly easy plants to grow and take kindly to being grown in captivity, whether in a greenhouse, conservatory, or indoors. *C. woodii*, often sold in garden centers and flower shops, makes a good hanging-basket plant, having little purple, green, and gray heart-shaped leaves. Often the hanging, vining stems make aerial tubers that can be taken off with a little of the vine attached and rooted to make further plants. The flowers are always upward turned and are like little, inverted parachutes; the petals are united for most of their length, only parted for the last 20 percent, but often rejoined again at the very tip: The pollinators have got to be able to get into the flower to do their job.

C. ampliata is a large-flowered, vining species that is thoroughly recommended. Flowering takes place rather late in the year. The flowers are mostly white with green tips to the petals.

C. haygarthii is another popular vining species from the eastern Transvaal, with medium-sized, flat-topped parachute flowers. *C. sandersonii* is similar but has much larger flowers.

One quite common but very different species is *C. stapeliiformis* from eastern

Ceropegiea ampliata is a large-flowered vining species that flowers late in the year.

Cape Province. The stems on this plant may be upright when very young, but it soon falls over and starts clambering up whatever is available. The stems are mottled brown and gray, and get very thin as the plant prepares to flower. This is a very robust species, but a little brittle at times, so plenty of cuttings are usually available.

There are more species that could be recommended; most are relatively easy. Propagation is by cuttings or from seed.

Conophytum

(Aizoaceae)

Conophytums come from southern Africa and Namibia, often growing on quartz patches of ground, in depressions in rocks, and in rock crevices. They have taken leaf succulence a degree further than lithops: What were the upper sides of flat leaves are almost totally united. Only a small slit remains to denote that each head is formed from two leaves. Some conophytum leaves are not so united, and these are referred to as "bilobes" because they have two distinct leaves that are usually united for half their length.

In the 1990s a complete revision of this group of plants took place, and *Conophytum* now includes: *Conophytum*, *Berrisfordia*, *Herreanthus*, and *Ophthalmophyllum*.

Conophytums are perhaps easier to grow than lithops; they are less likely to rot through overwatering or being left in less than favorable conditions. Their growing and resting periods are slightly different to lithops; in the northern hemisphere conophytums need to be rested for the first six months of the year, with one watering during March. They have to go through the same process as lithops: production of a new leaf pair and reduction of the previous leaf pair by absorbance by the new heads. During the resting period it is advisable to take conophytums out of direct sunlight, perhaps placing them under the bench in a greenhouse, otherwise they may get too hot and cook in their resting bodies. Once they start to grow again in July they must be brought into good light again.

The individual leaf pair of a conophytum is called a "head." These "heads" are usually much smaller than those of lithops, in some species they are not much bigger than a matchstick head, while in others they may be 2½ in. (6.5cm) long; they are usually a shade of green, and often spotted; the bilobes and other keeled species often have a red margin running along the keel; there is often a thin, darker green line surrounding the fissure, which is a small window.

Conophytums are quite capable of producing between three and seven new heads from the previous year's single head. This will depend on the species; the bilobes, being somewhat larger, are the types likely to generate the most heads. It does mean that a large mound of heads can be achieved in a relatively short time. It is important to keep the old leaf litter

Conophytum lithopsoides, a very soft-bodied plant flowering profusely in early autumn.

tidied away from the new heads, although this can be a tedious pastime. As you may imagine, these little heads afford many nooks and crannies in which pests can multiply.

These little jewels are propagated either by seed sown in a sandy loam mixture and not covered, or by taking cuttings after the resting period. Each individual head can be made into a cutting and should root within fourteen days, if the soil is kept slightly moist. Mist spraying the cuttings and seedlings is a good idea as it avoids the soil becoming too waterlogged.

The flowers on these enchanting little gems of plants are really worth waiting for; they can flower within one to two years of the seed being sown. The flower colors range from white to cream to pink to magenta to purple to yellow, orange, and red or mahogany. Not only do conophytums have a much greater flower color range than lithops, but unlike lithops there are nocturnal-flowering species. Their flowers tend to have much thinner petals and are usually a straw color;

but a few have pink flowers. One advantage the nocturnal-flowering species have over the other species is the very strong and exquisite perfume they exude. This attracts nocturnal pollinators, moths probably, who rely on their sense of smell rather than sight to direct them to their food sources.

Recommended day-flowering species are *Conophytum wettsteinii* with relatively large, flat-topped, pale green, unspotted heads and purple flowers; *C. taylorianum* with green, keeled, spotted heads and pale purple flowers; and *C. bilobum* with two distinct lobed leaves to each head, unspotted, sometimes with a red keel, and yellow flowers. *C. frutescens* is another bilobed species with slightly thinner leaves and orange flowers. *C. incurvum* var. *leucanthum* completes the trio, as this is another bilobe, but this time with white flowers. *C. globosum* is, as the name suggests, round headed, spotted, and has pale purple flowers. *C.* x *marnieri-anum* is a very easily grown plant, a naturally and unnaturally occurring hybrid that is quite variable in its body markings and flower colors; the flowers range from yellow through orange to purple. *C. ectypum* var. *tischleri* is a lovely species with large

Top:
Conophytum x "Shukuden."

Above:
Conophytum spectabile, a heavily scented species.

Below:
Conophytum x marnierianum, a naturally occurring hybrid.

golden flowers. *C. pellucidum* has a multitude of forms with no two plants being identical, but it is the flowers that really do put the icing on the cake as they are a pristine white with a small egg-yolk yellow center; a few forms do have pale pink/ purple flowers. This last species, *C. pellucidum,* is one to acquire once some of the others have been mastered.

Of the nocturnal-flowering species the following are recommended: *C. spectabile* with a darkish green body with red lines and spots on the upper parts, flowers are a medium-purple color with a heavenly perfume; *C. obcordellum* var. *ceresianum,* flat topped with some red spots and lines and a pale pink flower; *C. truncatum* with larger head than either of the previous two species, slightly spotted and with straw-colored, scented flowers.

The popularity of these plants with the people of Japan has induced hybridization of a number of the species. These are inter-generic hybrids with Anglicized Japanese names which are variously misspelled. Often orange-flowered plants are produced by hybridizing yellow- and purple-flowered species, although this is not always the case. Another characteristic, which has developed in the hybrids, is a whorling of the flowers, like a pinwheel.

These recommendations will get you started on the road to growing this charming group of plants and further involvement with them will mean contacting specialist nurseries and groups.

Cotyledon
(Crassulaceae)

This small genus of around ten species originates mostly in southern Africa. Winter growing and flowering, these plants can have hairy or smooth leaves, round or pointed, disc shaped or egg shaped. Often the plants are quite variable within one species, and may have plain green leaves, whitish leaves (with a farina) and may have a red margin around the leaves.

One of the smaller species and therefore suited to a small greenhouse or conservatory is *Cotyledon ladismithensis*. This is one of the hairy-leaved varieties and flowers quite easily with bell-shaped orange flowers. It forms a small bushy plant and is easily propagated from cuttings. *C. eliseae* has only recently been named, having been around for a number of years as the "cotyledon from Quartz River canyon." Smaller than *C. ladismithensis*, it has glutinous hairs on the leaves, every particle of soil sticking to the leaves when it is being repotted! *C. eliseae* with deep orange flowers makes a suitable subject for a hanging basket.

C. orbiculata has many forms, most having a bluish-white appearance to the leaves with a red margin. There is a form around without the attractive hue to the leaves, but this is much less common. An attractive species to grow, it is easy to cultivate from cuttings or leaves; the flowers are bell shaped with the tips of the orange petals, splaying outward.

Cotyledon ladismithensis is one of the smaller species and is suitable for a small greenhouse or conservatory.

Crassula
(Crassulaceae)

A very large genus containing some 200 species coming from the southern hemisphere, predominantly South Africa, but even found in Australia and New Zealand. They are very variable plants ranging from those which are hardy and suitable for the rock garden, the ground-hugging *Crassula sediforme*, to those which are aquatic, *C. helmsii*, and to plants such as *C. ovata*, which can reach a height and width of up to 8 ft. (2.5m).

They are for the most part easy to grow and propagate, predominantly by cuttings, although they can be raised from seed, which is very fine. Many species like to grow and flower in the winter months in the northern hemisphere, but they still look quite attractive even when they are not in full growth. The following plants are easily located or recommended.

C. ovata has had a variety of names and can still be found in garden centers and nurseries under most of them; *C. argentea* and *C. portulacea* are the other two Latin names often used, but there is also a variety of common names, including: Tree of Happiness, Jade Tree, Money Plant, Penny Plant, and Chinese Rubber Plant. Its habitat is Natal and Eastern Cape Province in South Africa.

C. ovata must be the most popular crassula, being propagated from cuttings very easily and frequently. It has glossy, dark evergreen leaves, and sheds its oldest leaves when it is neglected, for it then needs to conserve moisture and food. It flowers, budding up in late autumn and opening the flowers in midwinter. The flowers are star-shaped, with white petals that have a tinge of pink; although the individual flowers are small they are arranged in bunches all over the plant and can make quite a show. Much of the beauty of this plant lies in the massive trunk it produces with age, very treelike. It can be a problem finding a container large enough to accommodate this plant, but should it begin to get too large, then strike another plant and keep that in reserve against the day when the original plant becomes unmanageable.

These plants command very high prices in garden centers, sometimes quite astronomical prices considering the rapidity with which these plants can grow if fed and watered continuously.

The delightful *Crassula nealeana* in flower.

C. arta, or should this be called *C. cornuta*, *C. deceptor*, *C. deceptrix*, or *C. deltoidea*? It is a shame that there has been and still is so much confusion over this species, for it is very attractive and small growing. Certainly all of the plants described under these names are closely related and it may be that the variability is due to the different areas they come from, although all are from South Africa.

The habit of these little succulents is to stack their white, paired leaves alternately up a very short stem. The leaves are mostly spotted, but this is difficult to determine because of the very whiteness, which is a type of coating on the leaves, not a farina as it cannot be wiped off. Do not overwater these plants; they are slow growing and so need to dry out between waterings, have a well-drained compost, and good light.

Another crassula worthy of gracing a collection is *C. falcata*, also know as *Rochea falcata*. It has rough, bluish-gray leaves that look very like airplane propeller blades; technically the leaves are falcate or sickle shaped. This plant will reach 12–18 in. (30–45cm) in height, and even taller, once it is in flower as the inflorescence rises a further 6–8 in. (15–20cm) above the leaves. The deep coral red flower head is quite large and as an

Although *C. ovata* does enjoy being taken outdoors for the summer, it is not essential to do this to encourage flowering; the plant does keep a better shape if given maximum sunlight. As a houseplant *C.ovata* is often found growing in poor light and getting rather etiolated, until the distance between the leaf pairs becomes too great and the smaller branches begin to bend and look weak. This is not a subject for the bathroom, a dark hall, or similar place; it will not die if kept there, but neither will it look robust. There are other forms with different leaf colors: "Blue Haze" or "Blue Bird" (blue leaved—not the same as *C. arborescens*) and "Hummel's Sunset" with gold and red coloring in the leaves which is really brought out in strong sunlight. A further variety is "Crosby's Compact," like *C. ovata* but with smaller leaves, and a little slower. It still makes quite a large plant with age.

Closely resembling *C. ovata* is *C. arborescens*—it has the same mode of growth, although is not so fast growing. This plant comes from Western Cape Province in South Africa, a drier area than the habitat of *C. ovata*. Its main differences are the leaf color, which is blue with a red margin, and round leaves, whereas *C. ovata* has mostly ovate leaves. The leaves are also thicker on *C. arborescens*.

The delightful little *C. nealeana* from South Africa first came to prominence in the early 1930s. It is unlikely to grow beyond a 4½ in. (11cm) pot, but is easily pruned if it does get too big. Easy to cultivate from cuttings, this plant has small, bluish, opposite pairs of leaves with a red edge. It flowers in the autumn with a white, branched inflorescence, the backs of the petals being red.

added bonus is heavenly and heavily scented. Once the plant has flowered, it should shoot from the base and the top of the plant; it is at this point it may be better to start the plant again from one of the young shoots.

C. mesembryanthemopsis, rather a long name for a little plant, is so called because it resembles a mesembryanthemum. This is one of the smallest crassulas and one of the most attractive. It has bluish white, triangular leaves with flattened tips formed in a rosette, tightly hugging the ground. Note: Whenever a plant hugs the ground, it is worth giving it extra drainage in the soil to combat the moisture collecting around the neck of the plant; to keep the leaves from having contact with the soil it is a good idea to put a layer of coarse sand or small gravel between the leaves and the

soil. It grows in the autumn-winter-spring months making its flower clusters, which are white and sit in the center of the rosette, in autumn.

C. x "Morgan's Beauty" is a hybrid between the previous two plants and has somehow managed to select the best characters of both parents. It has the bluish-gray rough leaves of *C. falcata*, but has the compactness of *C. mesembryanthemopsis*. Flowering it falls midway between the two, having a pink cluster of highly scented flowers in the center of each head or rosette. This is is an absolute must have.

C. nemorosa from South West Cape Province in South Africa is an unusual little crassula. It grows from tiny underground tubers and in late summer to early autumn the little tubers send up small

Crassula plegmatoides on a rockery in South Africa with the quartz stones it would be growing near to in its natural habitat.

bluish-gray stems with small heart-shaped leaves. During the late autumn, if the plants are watered enough, the stems produce relatively large bell-shaped, creamy-white flowers. It is important that these plants are allowed to rest during the summer; during this time all the top growth dies down. We are sure that many pots of these tubers have been discarded because the owners believed them to be dead, when the tubers were merely resting.

Repotting can be a bit of a problem if undertaken while the plants are dormant. It is better to do it when they are just into growth; or, failing that, give them a good feed and forget about repotting the plants altogether. Propagation is from potting the little tubers which multiply readily.

C. muscosa, formerly named *C. lycopodioides* and will still be found with that name, is another easily acquired plant. It comes from Southwest Africa and is available in many forms. Its more usual habit is a small bush with stems 8–16 in. (20–40cm) tall and ⅛–½ in. (3–10cm) in diameter—in other words it is tall and skinny. The leaves are close packed round the stem, covering it completely. The flowers are yellow and so small that you may be forgiven for missing them if your plant has flowered. However there is a strange smell—it cannot be called a perfume—the flowers exude when they are open.

This is a very variable species. Some plants are so tiny that they really do resemble patches of moss for which this plant is named. There are variegated forms, cristate, and, more usually, monstrose forms. Cultivation is easy from cuttings.

C. marnierana and *C. rupestris* are plants which are seen quite frequently. Not difficult, they have a common name of jade necklace plant.

Some other crassulas recommended are *C. columnella*, *C. barklyi* (until recently known as *C. teres*), *C. pyramidalis*, and *C. quadrangularis*, each of which has an upright habit, often only clumping with age and having densely stacked pairs of leaves. When these plants flower that is the end of that particular head, so unless there are shoots at the base or adventitious shoots appear on the stem after flowering, the plant is lost. The flowers appear in tufts on the crown of the plant and are usually sweetly scented.

Further recommendations are *C. tecta* and *C. alstonii* (very choice); these plants have their flowers on longer flower spikes and they are held in bunches like a pompon. They are both whitish in appearance and do not like being overwatered.

Finally, three crassulas which make statuesque plants without getting too tall, up to 15 in. (38cm): *C. conjuncta*, *C. sladeniana*, and *C. perforata*. All are easily propagated from cuttings.

Dasylirion
(Nolinaceae)

This large-growing, small genus of plants is capable of attaining a diameter of 10–13 ft. (3–4m) in its natural habitat in the southern United States and Mexico. Dioecious and monocarpic, it is even more dependent than some plants on synchronized flowering. Like the agaves, this rosette-forming plant gathers itself for flowering, then dies after producing copious amounts of seed.

Dasylirion wheeleri is the most common species, with narrow, 2 ft. (60cm) long leaves, thin in cross-section, the leaves having fine teeth along the margins, which point toward the center of the plant (making it difficult to withdraw a hand should it have ventured in that far). The flower spike attains a height of 9 ft. (3m) and is plumelike in appearance. The seeds are tightly packed in the pods and are small, black discs. As with the agaves, the seeds are often heavily parasitized in the wild by the very insects that help to pollinate them, but it has such copious amounts of seeds that there is usually enough to satisfy all needs. We have had this plant survive successfully outside in winter in our garden.

Dudleya
(Crassulaceae)

These New World succulents come from California, Arizona, and Mexico. Rosette forming and usually with farinose leaves (white mealy substance), they are highly attractive plants. The leaves are easily marked, however, and once the white farina has been wiped or scraped off the leaf's surface, it doesn't regrow. The farina helps the plants retain moisture in their leaves, and not lose it through evaporation. In the wild this farina will be partially dispersed by heavy rains, but these usually come when the plant is dormant and the rosettes are partly closed.

Dudleyas, unlike echeverias, do not shed their lower, dried-up leaves, but tend to hang on to them, perhaps as protection for the stem. They grow during our summer and flower toward the end of it, and have many small, greenish-yellow, star-shaped flowers on one or two long flower stems. The smaller the species the more flower stems it will have. These plants do not have to be kept particularly warm in the winter, but do not like to get frosted.

Individual dudleya rosettes can attain a diameter of 18 in. (50cm), although not all the species grow this large.

Dasylirion wheeleri, the most commonly grown species of this genus.

Dudleya brittonii and *D. anthonyi* are two species that get big. Usually they do not offset, but have one very large head of leaves.

For the serious collector the fat-leaved *D. pachyphytum* is a must-have plant. It, too, has the white farina, with leaves as fat as fingers at times. It comes from Mexico and is rather slow, whether from seed or from cuttings. Cuttings, however, may be a long time coming as a plant would either need to have its center cut out to induce shooting or be divided up once it has begun branching dichotomously, usually after flowering.

D. farinosa is one of the smaller-growing species, which may be freely obtained. It has many small leaves 2½ in. (6cm) long and ¾–1¼ in. (2–3cm) broad. Other small-growing species recommended include: *D. cymosa* and *D. saxosa*.

For something completely different try *D. viscida*; this plant has long narrow leaves, without the farina. Instead it has a viscid or glutinous covering on the leaves, and all manner of small objects from soil particles to small insects become attached to the leaves and act as a protection in much the same way as the farina does for the other species.

Echeveria

(Crassulaceae)

These members of the Crassulaceae are much more widely dispersed than are the former genera but are still New World succulents. Their range is from the southern United States through Mexico and Central America down into Argentina. They are easy to cultivate, easy to hybridize, and easy to propagate—a beginner's dream. Some of the plants are unkindly referred to by hardened cactophiles as "cabbages" or "Brussels sprouts"; indeed some of the hybrids do have very large crinkly leaves.

These very accommodating plants are used in several ways: for carpet-bedding plants, for summer planting in containers in the garden, planted through a chicken-wire shape to be suspended from a pergola or hanging-basket hook, and grown in pots in a greenhouse.

There are 100 to 150 species and a lot more hybrids. They can have plain green leaves, hairy leaves, purple leaves, blue leaves and like the dudleyas, some even have a white farina. They are rosette forming and freely flowering throughout the year, often sending up flower spikes more than once in the year. The flowers range from pure lemon-yellow to bright scarlet and many species have bicolored yellow and orange or yellow and red flowers.

New species of Echeveria are still being discovered; they cover such a wide area with high mountain chains that it is almost impossible for every nook and cranny to have been explored for plants. Also it usually takes time to establish whether a plant that has been found is new or merely a new location for an existing species.

Hybrids abound and are not usually grown for the flowers but for the leaf form or color. Many have their origins in the United States, and have been deliberately hybridized, although some must have happened spontaneously in enthusiasts' collections when different species have flowered at the same time. Not only are there interspecific hybrids (*Echeveria* x *Echeveria*), but also there are intergeneric hybrids between *Echeveria* and *Graptopetalum* = *Graptoveria*; *Sedum* = *Sediveria*; *Dudleya* = *Dudleveria*; *Pachyphytum* = *Pachyveria*.

Many of the species of Echeverias can be found in garden centers and nurseries. *Echeveria agavoides*, so named because the rosette resembles an agave,

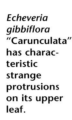

Echeveria gibbiflora "Carunculata" has characteristic strange protrusions on its upper leaf.

is a favorite. The leaves are pointed, but not dangerous, usually plain green but if the more recently reintroduced material is available then the leaves may have a red margin. The plants are often solitary and the rosettes may reach 12 in. (30 cm) in diameter. Closely related to this species is *E.purpusorum*. It is smaller headed and not so fast growing, but is has lovely purple flecking to the leaves.

E. elegans is a commonly found bluish-leaved species that will offset and provide the grower with a constant supply of plants. A somewhat larger bluish-leaved species is *E.gibbiflora* "Carunculata." The leaves on this plant have, when the plant is in full growth, a strange protuberance on the upper surface of the leaf, not unlike the wattle of a turkey; perhaps it is better described as a series of blisters. This outgrowth is not hollow. During the winter months when the leaves are not growing so fast this aberrance (or should it be abhorrence?) may subside and the leaves return to "normal."

E.pulidonis is a favorite yellow-flowered species with blue leaves with a red margin and the individual heads do not get too large, 3½ in. (9cm) in diameter, but it does clump in time.

Of the heavily farinose (white mealy surfaced) species, *E. subridgida*, which can attain the size of a large-headed dudleya, is a desirable species. It is, however, a little more difficult, for it has a tendency to rot off at ground level and then is not easy to re-root. It usually has a single rosette and does not normally offset, although cutting the center out may make it shoot, better to obtain some seed and raise more plants that way.

E. laui, from Mexico, is perhaps the species with the thickest leaves. It also has a white farina over them, and there is a most attractive flower spike with large powdery white bracts protecting the flowers. *E.runyonii*, from Mexico, is another heavily farinose plant. The leaves on this species are raised in the middle, in cross-section they are like an inverted V, and slightly curved, which adds a contrast to a collection.

A small crinkly edged leaf species with bluish-gray/pink leaves is *E. shaviana*. This is not a large-growing species, keeping to a 4 in. (10cm) pot quite happily for some time. This one can be a somewhat finicky grower.

Of the hairy species *E. setosa* must be a favorite, sending out hairy flower spikes with yellow and red flowers. This species does clump up and the offsets may be removed to make more plants and to keep the original to a manageable size. *E.leutotricha* is perhaps the most densely haired species, but perhaps a little more difficult to obtain.

With the exception of *E. leucotricha* and *E. gibbiflora*, the species discussed so far are stemless. Many of the hybrid echeverias will grow quite a tall stem in time. If this becomes too much of a totem pole, then the remedy is simple: cut the rosette off the stem at a reasonable height, leave to dry and callous over for a few days, and then pot up in a sandy soil mixture to root. This is best done at the beginning of the growing season, but can be done as late as August and still get the plant established before the winter. Do not throw the stock or bare stem away as this should send out shoots up and down the stem and so give you more progeny.

E. x "Katella" is one hybrid plant that has become too large in the past and has had the treatment described above. It is now virtually stemless and close to 24 in. (60cm) across. The single head has achieved this size by being regenerated and never having been allowed to flower: Every time a flower spike was visible near the center of the plant and it was big enough, I removed it. In

Above:
Echeveria subrigada is one of the most desirable plants in this genus.

Opposite
Echeveria x "Katella."

this way all the growth went into the plant and not into producing flowers and seed.

On a lot of echeverias it is possible to remove the larger of the flower bracts carefully and set them in sandy soil to root and produce young plants. Taking off the lower leaves from underneath the rosette and setting them in sandy soil may increase your stock of echeverias. Plants gained in these ways will be genetically identical to the parent plants.

There is no doubt that a massed collection of echeverias is a very colorful sight at any time of the year. These plants do need constant attention as they are terribly prone to mealy bug or white woolly aphid. Clear away all the old leaf remains to help control them, and repot the plants regularly. Only when the plants are moved do all the hiding places for these pests become apparent:

they always mass on the side of the plant that is not seen so much. Control of these pests can be biological, by using rubbing alcohol on a paintbrush, by picking them off with tweezers or your fingers, and by using insecticides. If you use insecticides, then please read the instructions. Do not spray the plants with the mixture as the Crassulaceae are sensitive to the spray and mark easily, especially the heavily adorned species. The best course of action is probably watering the soil with a systemic insecticide during the plant's growing cycle. (Systemic insecticides are not designed to work when the plant is not in growth).

For their soil requirements, echeverias are not terribly fussy. However, a sandy soil-based compost is the best option as it is easier to moisten after the winter dry rest, and is heavier than a peat-based compost and will therefore act as ballast for the plants, which can get top-heavy in their pots. It is necessary on occasion to weight down the pot by putting large pebbles around the top of the pot. To get maximum color into these attractive plants, they can be placed outdoors for the summer, but the waxy, farinose-leaved plants are better left under protection in case there is a sudden downpour, which will spoil the leaves.

Euphorbia
(Euphorbiaceae)

Euphorbias are part of an absolutely enormous family of some 300 genera and 8,000 species. They are to be found almost everywhere in the world: as highly succulent plants, small weeds, trees, rock plants, herbaceous plants, and seashore plants.

Their common name is the milkweed or spurge, and as the former name suggests, they have a milky sap which, when cut or damaged, bleeds or oozes out of the plant. Some species of the succulent euphorbias are under extreme pressure when they are in full growth, so the sap can spurt out in any direction. Warning: Be careful not to get this milky sap in an open wound, your eyes or any other vulnerable part of your anatomy. Should this happen accidentally, then wash the affected area with cold, clean water repeatedly and consult your doctor or local hospital emergency center if swelling occurs. The plant should also be doused in water to stop the sap from leaking. Do not be so alarmed that you will not

consider growing these plants. Care is all that is required.

There are probably at least 1,200 succulent species of euphorbia to choose from for your collection. Both succulent species and nonsucculent species have the same reproductive parts. It takes two to tango as they say, and both male and female flowers are needed to complete the process. In some species this means having two plants (at least), and in other species one plant has both male and female flowers.

Euphorbia pulcherrima is a good and well known plant to use to illustrate the flower structure of the euphorbia. Never heard of *Euphorbia pulcherrima*? How about poinsettia, the houseplant that epitomizes Christmas in the northern hemisphere? Those lovely large red, white or pink "petals" are in fact not petals but rather colorful bracts; the flowers do not have petals. The seed pod when it develops will have three chambers and only three seeds, if they have all developed properly. Flowering however does continue throughout the year, given a high enough temperature in the winter.

The second most well known euphorbia houseplant must be *E.milii*, the crown of thorns euphorbia. This is a succulent, although it is also quite woody stemmed and

Euphorbia obesa, from southern Africa, is one of the more succulent euphorbias.

drops its leaves if underwatered. This plant is capable of reaching 12 ft. (3.5m) in height and as much across. If it outgrows its welcome as a houseplant, it can easily be pruned to a more manageable size, the cuttings being rooted in a sandy multipurpose compost. Provided it is kept in sufficient light *E.milii* should flower the year round. The usual bract color is scarlet, but white, yellow, and pink or pale red are available. Also on the original *E. milii* the bracts are rather small; more recently introduced hybrids have larger bracts and are more showy. It is possible to raise these from seed.

A holiday on the Canary Islands will introduce you to a number of other euphorbias growing in their natural environment: *E. canariensis* is one, 6–10 ft. (2–3m) high and the same or more across, each thicket being made up of many four-sided stems.

These do make good potted-plant subjects, but will eventually get rather tall. *E. atropurpurea, E. balsamifera, E. regis-jubae,* and *E. aphylla* are four other commonly occurring species, but these tend to grow into bushes and do not usually take well to pot culture. *E. mellifera* is a nonsucculent euphorbia that can be grown in a sheltered spot in southern England and similar climates, preferably with its back to something warm like a wall or conservatory glass. One other euphorbia, *E. tirucalli,* can be seen in the Canary Islands but does not occur there naturally; it has been introduced to gardens, from which in some areas it has escaped.

The more desirable and more succulent species tend to come from southern Africa and Madagascar.

The most succulent must be *E. obesa*. It has no spines and no leaves but has a round to cylindrical body, ribbed, and highly patterned or checkered and reminiscent of tartan fabric. This plant will not tolerate overwatering and requires full sun and well-drained compost. Male and female plants are needed for seed production.

Similar to *E. obesa* are *E. meloformis* and *E. valida;* the prime difference is that these plants produce their flowers on long green stalks that dry to light brown and remain on the plant after the flower is finished, giving the impression that the plant is horned. They produce offsets with age and make clumps, which we have not heard of with *E.obesa.*

E. bupleurifolia, E. horrida, and *E. stellaespina* are three South African species and favorites at plant shows; they all clump up with age, although *E. horrida* makes the larger plant of the three. They are all attractive and rewarding plants to grow.

There are many Madagascan species, most of which require greater than average heat during the winter months; the usual solution is a heater in the greenhouse or bringing them indoors. Those with a similar habit to *E. milii* but not reaching the same dimensions are *E. leuconeura, E. lophogona, E. neohumbertii, E. viguieri,* and *E.hislopii.*

Smaller, lower-growing species from Madagascar are *E. decaryi, E. capsaintemariensis,* and *E. francoisii.* These all have enlarged root stocks and need careful cultivation; on the other hand they do not need full sun, for they are quite happy in semi-shade.

One rather charming little bush euphorbia with very thin stems that reach 12 in. (30cm) in cultivation, is *E. antisyphilitica* from the United States and Mexico. In the wild this makes very large low bushes, but in cultivation it is fairly slow. It has sweet little pink and white flowers during the summer for quite a long period. This plant is unlikely to outgrow a six inch 6 in. (15cm) pot.

The most commonly occurring plants in garden centers are *E.trigonus,* with three-sided stems and small deciduous leaves, often with purple red markings on the stems, clumping, will get quite large; *E.mammillaris,* which usually has green stems and small flower stalk remains; and *E. ferox,* with flower stalks that harden to spines, clumping. There are sometimes others, such as *E. cooperi, E. resinifera,* and *E. grandialata,* but these are larger-growing species.

Also seen sometimes are plants of *E. ingens.* This makes a thick four-sided column and grows eventually into a tree 30–40 ft. (9–12m) tall. It can grow extremely fast.

Succulent euphorbias are not really grown for their flowers, but for the body forms, color, markings and spines. Variegated and cristate forms of some species are available for those who like something different and indeed variegate plants do add a little more color to an otherwise rather green group of plants. Only a very few names have been mentioned here; there are many more and there is a specialty group concerned with the growing of these plants. New varieties are being discovered all the time, particularly from the Indian continent. We suspect that there are many yet to be discovered and named from the South American continent.

Right: *Euphorbia cooperi* is one of the larger-growing species that is widely available.

Faucaria

(Aizoaceae)

This small group of plants is very easy to grow and very rewarding. They come from east and southeast Cape Province in South Africa. They are clumping, stemless, green-leafed plants, sometimes spotted, usually with a keel to the back of the leaf and usually toothed on the leaf inner margin. These teeth give the plants the appearance of a pair of tiger's jaws, so much so that the specific names reflect this. Often the leaves have a pinkish or reddish tinge to the teeth or keel: take note that the plants must be grown in good light to make this develop. The form of these plants is three or four pairs of leaves stacked alternately on top of one another, sometimes branching.

The flower color with one exception is yellow, the exception being *Faucaria candida* with white flowers. The flowers are large, up to 2 in. (5cm) in diameter, often swamping the individual heads. They are autumn/winter flowering; *F. candida*, if it flowers late in the year, can have quite a pinkish tinge to the petals. The cold weather seems to enhance the color as much as, if not more than, sunlight. Watering these plants should take place during late spring, summer, and autumn; they need very little rest and will not be harmed if they are accidentally watered at other times. Repotting can take place whenever the plant

seems to need it, either because it has reached the edge of its existing pot or because it is looking sorry for itself.

Faucarias are prone to red spider mite, so keep a careful watch for this pest: telltale signs are a rusty appearance on the newer growth, or a very fine webbing over the center of the growths. Treatment is a proprietary insecticide from your local garden center. Propagation of these plants is easy either from seed, as with conophytums, or by cuttings.

Species to look for include *F. tigrina*, *F. felina*, *F. candida*, and *F. tuberculosa*, which as the name might suggest has warts on the upper surface of the leaves.

Gasteria

(Asphodelaceae)

Gasterias come from the coastal areas of South Africa, usually not penetrating more than 700 ft. (200m) inland. There are many names circulating for plants in cultivation, but only 16 distinct species are recognized, plus some subspecies.

Gasterias are most accommodating plants, wanting very little in the way of special treatment, except that they do not like being too cold and damp in the winter as this may cause black spots to appear

on the leaves; this is not life threatening but it will disfigure the plant until the affected leaves have grown out. Gasterias do need some water during the winter, but not too much. Try and boost the heat a little for them to avoid the black spots.

Gasterias get their name from the "swollen" base or stomach of each flower. The flowers are borne on a simple stem, or occasionally branched, and are usually green at the tip, followed by orange fading to yellow at the base. These plants are quite happy flowering at almost any time of the year, but the months when the light intensity is best are usually favored.

Soil requirements are again not highly critical, but it is advisable to include more sand than usual as the fleshy roots of these plants are apt to rot if insufficiently well drained.

Gibbaeum

(Aizoaceae)

Gibbaeums are a relatively small group of highly succulent plants that can be found in the southern Cape Province and Little Karroo in South Africa. They will be found growing where there are quartzitic patches or outcrops for the most part and they like extremely high light intensity.

The main distinguishing feature of these plants is the unequal length of the two leaves, which are almost united except when flowering or producing a

new pair of leaves. In shape, apart from the lack of teeth, they are very reminiscent of a shark's jaw.

With a few exceptions, these plants are pubescent to a lesser or greater extent, which acts as protection against the brilliance of their surroundings and gives them a silvery-white appearance. Many species are low growing with just two species becoming taller: *Gibbaeum pubescens* and *G.pachypodium*, although there is less tendency for them to elongate in the wild. Those without hairs are *G. petrense*, *G. comptonii*, *G. heathii*, *G. luckhoffii*, and *G. gibbosum*. A few species have much longer leaves and are scarcely united at all: *G. haagei*, *G. schwantesii*, and *G. velutinum*.

Many growers find these plants shy to flower, partly because each has its own set growing time and cannot be made to grow at any different time. Also, the majority tend to want to flower during the time of year when we have our shortest days and fewest hours of sunshine. However, count it as an achievement if you do manage to get them to flower. The flower colors are either white or more usually purple. There is a plant in circulation that looks like *G. velutinum* with an orange flower, which is a hybrid with a glottiphyllum. Propagation is from seed or cuttings.

Greenovia

(Crassulaceae)

This is another charming little succulent genus from the Canary Islands off the west coast of Africa. There are only two or three species and they are all equally easy to grow.

Greenovia dodrantalis is perhaps the best species to recommend because it offsets freely. *G.aurea* tends to stay solitary, which can be disastrous should the only head decide to flower as it is a terminal inflorescence.

These ground-hugging, blue-gray, glaucous-leaved plants are winter growing. During the summer months when they are resting the rosettes of leaves close up, looking for all the world like a blue rose bud; but come the autumn and some moister, cooler weather and the "buds" begin to open up. Flowering, when it does occur, is at the end of the winter or early spring. We have never found seedlings appearing spontaneously from these plants and must therefore deduce that they are self sterile.

We have recently planted some three or four plants outdoors on a rockery in a sheltered position; although they have had some frosts, so far they are alive and thriving. The test will come if we get snow and it lays on the crowns of the plants. As a safeguard, give some protection in the form of fleece, bracken, or a pane of glass propped up.

Left:
Greenovia dodrantalis from the Canary Islands.

Below:
Haworthia minima, a delightful clump-forming species with thick leaves.

Haworthia

(Asphodelaceae)

Haworthia, a genus of some 70 species, originates in southern Africa. This genus tends to grow in the winter in the northern hemisphere. The species are generally low growing, rosette forming, and clumping. Leaf shape ranges from truncate and windowed to almost grass-like. The growing medium for these plants should have an additional measure of sharp sand or potting grit, as many of them have enlarged, fleshy roots which can rot quite easily if overwatered. Although these plants are free-flowering the flowers are nothing to eulogize over. They are borne on a thin stem 4–12 in. (10–30cm) tall and are mostly white-cream with perhaps a hint of pink. They hybridize among themselves, and some interesting offspring have developed on occasion. Generally though, hybridizing these little succulents only causes more confusion.

Haworthia attenuata fa. *clariperla* is one of the most attractively marked species, and quite easy to grow. It offsets well and can therefore be given to admiring friends. The white horizontal lines on the back of the dark green leaves are usually quite well raised.

H. *minima* is a delightfully marked species, clump forming with thick leaves with more or less pronounced white tubercles. It is not very fast growing and is worth keeping the clumps intact. Remember, it is always prudent to remove one offset and pot it to keep as a reserve plant against losing the main plant.

H. *venosa* fa. "Coriacea." This particular form is a very large-leaved form of what is sometimes still called H. *tesselata*. This whole group of haworthias is very well-marked with their square or tesselate patterns on the leaf surfaces. This is a very good species with which to begin a collection.

There are many "retuse" species of haworthia, and they are a delight to behold. These highly windowed varieties take on an exceedingly glossy appearance when they are fully turgid and a somewhat more matte-like appearance when they are resting. A few varieties to look for are H. *comptoniana*, H. *retusa* (and varieties), and perhaps the best of all—H. *emelyae*.

One of the most attractively marked haworthia, *H. attenuata* fa. *clariperla.*

Hoya
(Asclepiadaceae)

The common name for hoyas is wax flowers. The 90 or so species range from Indonesia and the surrounding area to the Himalayas. Often they are epiphytic and are twining or vining plants. They are highly attractive to mealy bug aphids, for the plants exude large amounts of nectar from their flowers and leaf axils. Some species have very tough, persistent leaves, while others have smaller, thinner leaves that are shed if the conditions are too sunny or too dry. Many can grow to whatever size you want. All the species we have had the privilege to see flowering were very sweetly scented.

In the wild, hoyas are accustomed to protection from much larger plants or trees, and therefore often live in semishade. Consequently they make very good house plants. The most commonly grown species is *Hoya carnosa*, but it does not live up to the common name, as the individual flowers—and there may be 20 to 30 in each individual umbel or bunch—are not waxy but are rather quite felted, with glasslike, raised coronas. With all of the hoyas, it is important that, once they have flowered, the flowering peduncle is not removed as the plants will continue to flower from the same peduncle repeatedly, the peduncle getting quite long with age.

H. *carnosa* comes in variegated forms and there is even a form with monstrose or deformed leaves. Often the two characteristics are combined.

Jatropha
(Euphorbiaceae)

This is a very large group of plants that are closely related to euphorbias, and in distribution are widespread throughout the tropics. Many species are available as they grow readily from seed, but just how many of them are succulent is debatable. Warning: Some of the more herbaceous plants have hairs or barbs on the stems and undersides of the leaves which, like stinging nettles in the UK, can cause a very nasty, inflamed rash to appear; some people react to the stinging hairs more strongly than do others.

We recommend only two: *Jatropha podagrica*, grown extensively in continental Europe as a houseplant and with scarlet flowers, both male and female flowers on the same stem; and *J. cathartica*, formerly known as *J. berlandieri*, the most succulent of them all, having a large underground, swollen stem; so it requires well-drained compost and care with watering.

H. bella is also often available as a houseplant and makes a good hanging-basket subject but, please note, it really does not like being in the sun at all. This little hoya has very glassy flowers and really does not look real; it is a delightfully perfumed species.

H. multiflora is another popular species. It is sometimes given the common name shooting rocket because the flowers have reflexed petals that make the flowers look as if they are little rockets.

H. cinnamomifolia looks remarkably like *H.carnosa* until it flowers. It has fewer flowers in the umbel, the petals are backward pointing, and the coronas are a dark cinnamon color.

It is doubtful that any of the hoyas can truly be considered as succulent, but

they are very close relatives of many similar plants and so creep in by association. If plants such as *H. carnosa* are considered succulent, then *Stephanotis floribunda* should also be included.

Propagation can be from seed but is more usually from cuttings.

Huernia
(Asclepiadaceae)

The huernias are among the easiest of the stapeliads to grow, and do not have unpleasant-smelling flowers. Most species are quite small but very free flowering. *H. namaquensis* var. *hallii* has pretty spotted flowers about 1 in. (2.5cm) in diameter. *H. primulina* has larger yellow flowers, and *H. boleana* bigger stems and larger flower with extended lobed petals. Many other interesting species and forms exist.

Above left:
Huernia primulina.

Below:
Heurnia namaquensis var. hallii.

Kalanchoe

(Crassulaceae)

Kalanchoe is a very large genus of plants containing over 200 species, or at least 200 names as some of these names are probably redundant and apply to similar plants described more than once by different people. They come from Madagascar, southern Africa, and extend into Arabia, beyond into India and further east.

Many species have become popular with enthusiasts, particularly those which are easy to propagate. Most available species will grow in the summer months, although flowering often takes place in the winter.

The most frequently sold species must be *Kalanchoe blossfeldiana*. It is often sold in florists' shops, chain stores, garden centers, and so on. This plant comes in a variety of flower colors from deep red to lemon yellow; the leaves are glossy green with notched edges. You must keep this plant in reasonably good light even when it is not in flower, otherwise it will not repeat its colorful display another year.

The "Oak-leaf" form of *Kalanchoe beharensis*.

K. tubiflora, also known as and recently reinstated as *Bryophyllum tubiflorum*, must be the world's most easily propagated plant. Every narrow leaf on this Madagascan plant is capable of producing, on average, eight new plants that will be identical to the parent plant. They develop as adventitious plantlets from around the leaf ends, sending roots out into the moist air, and when the leaf begins to wither, these adventitious plantlets fall to the ground or the top of the pot in which the parent is growing, and the roots then search for better nourishment by rooting down into the compost. The only way to rid your collection of this plant is to leave it outside for the winter to freeze. There are approximately 30 species in the group of kalanchoes that behave in this way for the most part. Most are not in general cultivation, but *K. diagremontanum* (deltoid-shaped leaves) and *K. rauhii* (leaf shape is between the other two) are two names that might be encountered.

K. tomentosa is another very popular species; its leaves are covered in white hairs with brown hairs at the tips. It forms a multi-stemmed plant and has to reach a height of 18 in. (45cm) to 2 ft. (60cm) before it will flower in the winter to early spring. The flowers are really not that spectacular, being a rather washed out creamy-brown. The beauty of this plant definitely lies in the leaves.

K. beharensis comes from southern Madagascar and with considerable age will become a tree. The leaves are densely covered with short hairs, slightly serrated, and deltoid in shape. When this plant is beyond the seedling or cutting stage and is being watered and fed frequently, the leaves can get quite large: 4–12 in. (10–30cm) long and 8 in. (20cm) broad. They are very tactile, thankfully harmless, and usually unharmed by being stroked or touched. Reminiscent of a donkey's ears, in full sun these leaves take on a lovely bronzed appearance on the upper surface. The new growth lacks this color being rather white/green, but as soon as the leaves have fully grown then they quickly develop their tanned appearance.

Several forms of this plant are available: a heavily lobed variety called the "Oak-leaf" form; a particularly dark-leaved variety, sometimes referred to as the "Chocolate" form; a form called "Fangs," which is hairy to the same degree but additionally has many warty excrescences on the underside of the leaves; and, if you do not like hairy plants there is even a "glaucous" or nude form.

It is very important to keep repotting these plants; if there is a danger that it is getting too big for you, then take the side shoots off, root them, keep one of them for yourself, then pass the other on to someone who has more room. Winter temperature is not too critical, although it will probably do best if kept to a minimum of 45°F (7°C), or a little higher.

K. rhombopilosa is a delightful little kalanchoe with gray chocolate-flecked leaves. The leaves are not terribly well attached to the stem of the plant and if handled at all roughly, the plant will shed many of its leaves. All is not lost, however, as all of the leaves will root readily. It does not like being cold in the winter and will need some water to prevent too many leaves shedding.

Some kalanchoes make excellent hanging-basket subjects, *K. pumila*, from central Madagascar, being one plant that comes to mind. It is primarily a winter grower and will flower in the early spring, often putting on an excellent display at Easter. The plant is about 6 in. (15cm) tall, consisting of many shoots arising from soil level. It has small, crenate, mealy white leaves that make a marvelous background for the pink flowers. Some water during the winter months will have to be given for this plant to flourish.

One more kalanchoe we would like to recommend is *K. thyrsiflora*. These plants come from South Africa: the Orange Free State, Natal, and Transvaal. Again though, it is predominantly winter growing and flowers in the early spring. This plant does branch with age or flowering, but does not grow too tall: 12 in. (30cm). The

Various leaf shapes and colors of *Kalanchoe beharensis*.

leaves, under greenhouse protection, are about 4 in. (10cm) in diameter and are almost round, but are very thin in cross-section. They have a white meal covering their surface which is easily wiped off by inquisitive fingers. In the wild this mealy appearance to the leaves is rarely present and the leaves are quite sunburnt looking, for the elements soon divest the leaves of their coating. The flowers are worth waiting for, although they are fairly small and lemon yellow; the perfume is so strong and exactly like Lily of the Valley plants that any conservatory or greenhouse will be swamped with the scent.

Unfortunately the plant usually dies after flowering and propagation must therefore be from seed, but sometimes the head that has flowered will produce a number of shoots, so these can be taken off and rooted. Do not overwater this plant.

Lampranthus
(Aizoaceae)

An easy genus of plants to grow, they will enjoy being bedded out for the summer and may be left out for the winter; do, however, take a couple of cuttings and put them under protection as a precaution against a bad winter.

These are subshrubs and can be erect, spreading, or prostrate and have many leaves. Flower color can be anything from white to pink to red to purple or rose, or orange to yellow. To see a bush of *Lampranthus aureus* with its bright orange flowers in full blossom is dazzling. There is no point in going through the species names, as they all flower well if given half a chance. Propagation is from seed or from cuttings.

Lithops
(Aizoaceae)

These "living stone" plants are firm favorites with would-be collectors and established collectors alike. They come from southern Africa, from very dry regions with very strong light intensity.

Each head of these stemless, highly succulent plants is comprised of a single pair of very fat leaves, referred to as a head. The upper surface of what might once have been a flat, thin leaf, has been forced to face its opposite leaf by the underside of the flat leaf swelling up with water-storing cells. The end of the flat leaf has then been truncated to form a window through which light is allowed to stream in order that the plant may photosynthesize.

Every year each head—and a plant may have more than one—produces a new pair of leaves, occasionally two pairs of leaves, from the center or between the two leaves. While these new bodies or heads are emerging and growing, the plants must be allowed to rest and must not be watered. Once the new bodies have fully

emerged and the old leaves have become papery thin or leathery, recommence watering. Note: It is important that these plants are never left standing in water; always let the surplus water drain right away.

Lithops plants much prefer a loam-based compost with added sand or grit, and very good drainage is essential. Repotting is best carried out at the beginning of their growing season: May or June in the northern hemisphere. Do not give them a rich compost to grow in; provided they are repotted or offsets are potted every three to four years, it should not be necessary to feed them. It is

Lithops bella, a white-flowered species that flowers in the autumn.

so easy to overfeed these highly succulent plants, but this weakens the epidermis, stretches it, and can cause the heads to rot off. Very little can be done when this occurs; with a multiheaded plant it may be possible to salvage one or two heads, but more often than not the fungus will have infected all the heads.

It is almost essential to have a greenhouse in which to grow these plants. However, we have seen some very well grown specimens in an apartment. The owner had a balcony and was able to put his plants outside for the summer without fear of them getting too wet or

slugs and snails attacking them. The plants were brought in before the weather became too cold and were put on a table right in front of the window. Trying to grow these plants on a window sill is not easy as many houses have double-glazed windows which cuts down considerably on the amount of useful light. But a single-glazed window should be satisfactory, if it is south or west facing.

Lithops do not like hot

humid conditions: they need cool nights in order to grow and flower well. Coolness also intensifies the leaf colors. It is not unknown for these plants to receive frost and snow in the wild, although it is not recommended that this particular weather condition be emulated in cultivation. In winter the plants really do not need to be kept particularly warm, 40°F (5°C) is all that is required. When they are growing during the late spring, summer, and autumn it is important to let them have plenty of air passing over their heads. Stagnant hot air is lethal to these plants, as the bodies will boil and you will be left with a mushy shell of a plant. A good idea for stirring up the air is to install a couple of fans from defunct computers at either end of the benching in your green-

house. It is far better to increase air movement than it is to put up shading over the greenhouse glass.

It is a pity that, when these charming little mimicry plants are offered for sale in garden centers, they are often displayed in a heavily shaded area. This only makes the plants "soft" and likely to rot, so it really is not in the best interests of garden centers.

The flowers on lithops are either white, yellow, or yellow with a white center and are produced toward the autumn. Some varieties of *Lithops pseudotruncatella* may flower as early as the end of June in the southern part of the UK. It is normal for the white-flowered species to flower later in the year.

Yellow-flowered species recommended for growing are *L. pseudotruncatella, L. aucampiae, L. hookeri,* and *L. lesliei.* White-flowering species recommended are *L. salicola* and *L. karasmontana.* Some cultivars are available with body colors

Above: *Lithops aucampiae,* a yellow flowered "stone plant."

Opposite: *Nolina recurvata,* the Ponytail Palm, is a good patio plant for frost free environments.

different from the usual species; for example *L. optica rubra*; normal *L. optica* has a grayish/green body but *L.optica rubra* has ruby red leaves. This phenomenon does make the cultivars more difficult to grow, so initially it might be better to ignore these and settle for growing the more normal forms.

Lithops are easily raised from seed provided that the seed is not covered or put in a dark place, as the Aizoaceae family needs light in order to stimulate germination. The seed-dispersal mechanism for many of this family is ingenious. The seed capsules develop after the plants have flowered and dry to a hard "bud." When the rains come this "bud" or capsule absorbs the moisture and opens up the "petals," more accurately valves, and the capsule looks for all the world like a flower opening. The seeds are then splashed out by the rain drops and fall to the ground; if the rain is not persistent, the capsule will close up and wait for more rain before opening again, when the conditions for germination of the seed should be better. The botanical term for this is hygrochastic.

Nolina
(Nolinaceae)

This genus of succulent plants originates mainly in Mexico. The plants are often to be found in garden centers, frequently with the common name ponytail cactus (*Nolina recurvata*) attached to them. They make very good houseplants and can stand outside for the summer months. The plants on sale have often had their centers deliberately removed or damaged to force them to produce many growing points or shoots; this occurs naturally with age but only after flowering. It has to be quite large to flower, say 3–4 ft. (1–1.25m) in height. Like the agaves, these plants need to be repotted regularly to attain a statuesque size.

Pachyphtum
(Crassulaceae)

Closely related to echeveria, pachyphytum comes solely from Mexico. There are some 12 species, and each of these is clump forming. They hybridize readily with echeveria, and we believe there is a hybrid with sedum.

The leaves of the rosettes are often quite tightly compacted, so much so that they impress their outline on the preceding and following leaves to make a mark on the leaf. The other genus of succulent plant in which this is encountered is agave. The leaves on most of the species are bluish with a dusting of farina in some species.

The plants flower freely with long, curved flower spikes with bell-shaped flowers, usually red or dusky pink. Large bracts encasing the individual flowers. There is usually a copious amount of nectar that can drip on other plants should they be nearby.

The species usually available are *Pachyphytum hookeri*, small leaved and compact growing; *P. glutinicaule*, with a sticky stem; *P. oviferum*, with the common name of sugared almond plant, a good visual description. It can range from quite a large mass of heads to a container 24 in. (60cm) across, but this takes some careful growing as the leaves are marked easily and repotting is somewhat difficult without doing some damage to the plant.

P. viride is a very robust, green-leaved species with greenish-white petals to the flowers and red inner parts. It is not that fast growing, but it will grow a little taller than some of the species, to about 12 in. (30cm) or so.

Pachyphytums are attractive and easily grown succulents.

Pachypodium
(Apocynaceae)

This genus of succulent plants has about 13 species which come from southern Africa and Madagascar. All require well-drained compost and no overwatering. Coming in various shapes and sizes, all have spines or thorns.

The two easiest and very similar species to grow are *Pachypodium lamerei*, with green shiny leaves, and *P. geayi*, with darker, narrower leaves. They are very suitable for indoor culture and can reach a height of 26 ft. (8m) in the wild, but a third of that height is more realistic under glass. Certainly *P. lamerei* will flower at 6 ft. (2m); the plant bears white, scented flowers at its crown. Similar to these two species, but from Namibia rather than Madagascar, is *P. namaquanum*, also known by its common name: half mans. This plant is much slower in growth and really does need a sunny spot in the greenhouse.

Other species requiring more care in their cultivation are *P. baronii* with light red flowers; *P. baronii* var. "Windsori," bearing bright red flowers; *P. densiflorum* with dark yellow flowers; *P. rosulatum*, with light yellow flowers; and *P. brevicaule* with chrome yellow flowers. Propagation for all of them is from seed.

Pedilanthus
(Euphorbiaceae)

The last genus in this large family that we consider worth mentioning is one that occurs in the garden center trade from time to time. Usually it is not displayed with the other cacti and succulents, but is placed with the houseplants, which gives us a clue as to the best conditions in which to grow it. The pedilanthus come entirely from the Americas, occurring mostly in Mexico, although it may simply be a question of plants not having been discovered and named.

Pedilanthus tithymaloides is the plant most often found offered for sale, and then in its variegated form. It is a jointed to the point of being a zig-zagging, many-stemmed plant with green, variegated leaves for about half its height. If it decides to flower, and this particular species seems somewhat shy, then the flowers will be red, to many people resembling a red bird.

P. macrocarpus is jointed but the joints stay more or less in a straight line reaching a height of 6 ft. (2m) without any trouble at all. It needs to be repotted regularly to keep it growing well and flowering; again the flowers are red and like small birds. This particular

species has very felted stems, which gives the stems a gray appearance, and very tiny ephemeral leaves; often this plant will produce monstrose growths, we believe because of accelerated growth. Given free root run, this montrose growth is even more abundant, although the flowering is less.

Propagation is from seed (three seeds to a pod) or cuttings. Cuttings seem to take a very long time to get going, often one to two years. Here is a trick we have been advised to try with any thin-stemmed succulents: tie several stems together with raffia or string and plant the bundle in a pot.

Piaranthus
(Asclepiadaceae)

The piaranthus have similar growth pattern to the duvalias and are also easy to grow, but the flowers are generally rather lighter in color than the duvalias and spotted. They do have a fairly unpleasant smell.

Pleiospilos
(Aizoaceae)

These chunky, granitelike, highly succulent plants come from the tablelands of the Little and Great Karroos and Cape Province in South Africa. They are a dark bluish-gray in color, finely and densely spotted, with a burnished red appearance if they are grown in full sun. They are easy plants to keep and fairly undemanding. With some species a pair of leaves can reach a combined length of 7–8 in. (18–20cm), although their width is not usually this great.

In the wild their existence has been successful because of their strong resemblance to their surroundings: the granitic rocks. In all probability the plants were a lot more diverse eons ago, but it is those which most closely resembled their surroundings that survived and produced further plants like themselves.

Pleiospilos nelii's natural habitat is the granite rocks of the southern part of South Africa.

The chunkiest of these plants, *Pleiospilos bolusii, P. simulans,* and *P. nelii,* normally have one pair of leaves although, like the lithops, they produce a new pair of leaves each year and the old pair is absorbed; so for a period there may be two sets of leaves stacked one on the other and at right angles. *P. compactus* and its varieties can have up to four pairs of leaves, usually less chunky and longer.

These plants grow for the latter half of the year in the northern hemisphere, so commence watering during July, provided the majority of the old leaves have dried up and become very leathery. Flower buds will appear during August and may be from one to five in number, coming from between the newest leaf pair, with the oldest bud in the center and the others either side in a line.

The flowers are quite large, getting bigger with each day that they are open; they are golden yellow in color with an orange tinge to the outermost petals. The petals "fade" to a reddish-orange and flop all over the leaves, so try to get them off the leaves by twisting them out of the way. After flowering, which can continue on into late autumn, the plants begin to push through new leaves from the same point as the flowers. At least one new head should appear, and if conditions have been good perhaps two heads will appear and so the plant will increase its size.

One species, *P. nelii,* does not normally flower until after Christmas, perhaps even February depending on the weather. The flowers actually come from the new heads; i.e., the plant produces the new body before budding up. This species also has much more rounded leaves than the others. The flower is a salmon-orange, but because of the lateness of the flower there is always the danger that it will not develop fully.

Propagation of these plants is usually from seed, but they will root from cuttings if necessary.

Sansevieria

(Dracaenaceae)

This extensive genus which comes from the African continent, has one representative, which must be in thousands of homes throughout the world and the owners probably do not even know they have a succulent: *Sansevieria trifasciata* or Mother-in-Law's Tongue! It can outgrow a 15 in. (40cm) pot quite quickly and can be divided regularly. This particular species comes in a variety of guises. The most boring is the plain, dark-green-leaved form. The variegated forms are more interesting, having either a yellow stripe down each edge of the leaf or a yellow stripe through the middle. The leaves usually have horizontal banding and these on occasion have been known to flower, although the flower spikes on these particular species are not huge. The flowers open in the evening and can be quite highly scented, like Hyacinth perfume. A more easily accommodated variety is *S. trifasciata* "Golden Hahnii," which has much shorter rosettes and proliferates more slowly.

Some varieties, i.e., *S. pinguicula*, have a habit of "walking" across the ground or on top of a pot, with their new offsets: they produce a stolon above ground and the plantlet on the end then puts down roots when it is a short distance from its parent. Some species such a *S. cylindrica* with cylindrical stems can be quite

slow growing. *S. grandis* is perhaps the largest-growing species, producing a flower spike up to 4 ft. (1.25m) tall. *S. aethiopica* is a small species that does very well in cultivation, offsetting and flowering easily, and it also has a quite large flower spike, again highly perfumed. All in all, this genus is a very long suffering one and will tolerate most conditions.

Sedum

(Crassulaceae)

A large number of species resides in this genus, commonly called the stonecrops, and they are very widespread throughout the world. The 600 or so species come from very varied habitats: Japan, China, Mongolia, Siberia, North America, Mexico, Peru, Morocco, and Europe. Specific species are suitable for rockeries, herbaceous borders, hanging baskets, and containers in greenhouses.

Some of the common hardy species suitable for the rockery are *Sedum kamtschaticum*, coming in plain or variegated leaf form with golden flowers; *S. spathulifolium*, a small-rosetted, white-leaved plant, the older leaves being denuded of their farina are a purple color; *S. populifolium*, which

dies down for the winter; *S. spurium*, an exceedingly common pink-flowered plant; yellow-flowered *S. rosea* in which the herbaceous parts die down to a gnarled rootstock or stump each winter.

S. spectabile, an absolute must for any garden with its umbels of pink flowers that are highly attractive to the last butterflies and bees of the year; similar to *S. spectabile* is *S. telephium* "Autumn Joy," but with less showy reddish flowers. These species are not generally accepted as succulent species.

Among the species recommended for hanging baskets under glass during winter, possibly to be moved outside for the summer, are the following: *S. morganianum*, the burro's tail sedum to use its common name, makes dense masses of hanging stems; good light is essential, otherwise the leaves will become even more loosely attached than they are usually. The one failing with this species is that the leaves are easily knocked off the stems. Every leaf that falls will send out roots and a new plant form, but a bare stem is the result. The red flowers are not very conspicuous, coming at the ends of the trailing stems. There is another similar plant but not quite so common, *S. burrito*; the leaves on this

species are smaller and more rounded and are not shed so readily.

S. sieboldii must be the sedum most frequently sold in shops and garden centers. It is extremely accommodating, and the color in the leaves is enhanced if kept in sunlight. Either out of doors, or in a porch or conservatory, the stems reach about 12 in. (30cm) long; the leaves are small almost round and flattened, glaucous, with varying amounts of red and pink in them according to the amount of light received. If this plant is grown outdoors permanently, then the stems will be shorter. The flowers are pink and appear in the autumn. Equally common is the variegated form, which is perhaps a little shier.

S. treleasei is an extremely common succulent plant from Mexico. The upright, unbranched stems attain a height of nearly 2 ft. (60cm), and there is a danger that, if it is not given enough good quality light, the stems will fall over or even break off under their own weight. The usual form is quite glaucous, but a more pruinose form, "Haren," is around. The flowers are borne on a flat-topped inflorescence.

S. lucidum is another commonly grown plant, although we suspect that it may be masquerading under the name of *S. x rubrotinctum*, perhaps even more common. *S.lucidum* is identical in habit but with smaller leaves and does not get so tall.

Of the more desirable species, or more commonly exhibited sedums, *S. suaveolens* is a good example. This particular species is very similar in appearance to *Echeveria subridgida* or one of the large-headed dudleyas: indeed when it is not bearing evidence of its flowers it is often mistaken for the former. The plant is stemless and often solitary, although it will clump with age, the individual heads reaching 9 in. (23cm) across before sending out stolons. The leaves are glaucous, and the flowers stems emerge from fairly low down on the plant and initially are indistinguishable from the stolons; the flowers are white with dark red anthers.

Delightful *S. hintonii* might be exhibited more it were it were not for the fact that it is chiefly winter growing and flowering. This small-growing plant with densely white bristly-haired blue leaves dies down after flowering.

Sedum lucidum, although not hardy, is commonly found in one of its color forms, which range from green to red to variegated.

Because this is an autumn/winter grower, it is important to give it a very little water during the worst months of the year, but on no account get any water on the leaves as they will rot, and the whole plant may be lost. Note: It is always worthwhile growing those plants that are susceptible to overwatering in clay pots or pans so that the compost dries out more quickly.

S. greggii is another widely grown, small species although it is often seen unnamed. This plant dies down in the resting period, after flowering in midsummer. New growth from the bases of the old flowering stems, is very cone-like in shape and pale green in color. These conelike new heads also occur along the length of the old flower stem and can easily be removed for propagation; indeed as the flower stem withers the growth buds drop off anyway.

S. craigii, with its bluish-pink leaves, has become more popular and will make a suitable subject for a hanging basket in the greenhouse. It, too, has white flowers. *S. furfuraceum* has become very widespread in collections and again might make a good hanging-basket plant; the leaves are small, dark green fading to red as the leaves mature; it has white flowers and is easily cultivated from cuttings.

S. palmeri is a plant worth trying outdoors on a rockery when you have enough plant material. It has blue, glaucous, thin, round leaves and forms clumps of stems. The flowers are yellow and borne on an arched inflorescence near the top of the stem.

Some sedums reach very large proportions, indeed they are referred to as the "tree sedums." *S. frutescens* is perhaps the most well known and often grown species, which can reach 3 ft. (90cm) at least in height. It really does have a trunk to it with papery bark, which is always in a state of peeling. This tan-colored bark is thick enough to write on with a ball-point pen, should the mood take you. The young stems are very brittle and will not stand being moved suddenly or knocked. They do become tougher with age however, and the pieces that are accidentally broken off root easily but do take a little time to take on their characteristic treelike appearance.

So many worthwhile species have to be omitted here through lack of space, but do look around your garden centers and nurseries for hardy species to try and also for some different species to try under cover. Go to specialty nurseries and alpine garden centers, and who knows what you may find?

Sempervivum
(Crassulaceae)

These hardy succulents occur naturally in alpine regions of North Africa and Europe. Ideally suited to rockeries, they can be too well treated if grown in pots, but please do not be put off from doing so. Whatever the situation they are being grown in, rock garden or succulent greenhouse, they need a very well-drained, soil-based compost with added potting grit. They also benefit from a top-dressing of small grit or fine gravel, to keep the leaves up above any damp conditions. Slugs and snails adore these juicy plants, but are somewhat selective, preferring the slower-growing, choicest plants.

With all sempervivums, the individual heads die after each one has flowered. Hopefully, long before they flower the plants will have produced many offsets or stolons. Occasionally, however, a plant may flower before reproducing vegetatively and unless seed is forthcoming that will be the end of your plant. If you have a several sempervivums, and two plants flower at the same time, there is a danger of them hybridizing. Perhaps danger is not the right word to use, as there are already many hybrids in cultivation, but so many of them are unfortunately unnamed and of unknown parentage. Sempervivums have been collected extensively. Since they propagate easily from offsets and root in days, it is not surprising that those first collected were passed around rapidly.

It is not unusual to find whole collections of these delightful little rosettes growing in pots on garage roofs. Indeed sempervivums can often be found growing on the roofs themselves, getting a tenacious toe-hold on life with their fine hairlike roots; they almost look like moss growing on the tiles.

Sempervivum rosettes range in size from ⅛–6 in. (5mm–15cm) in diameter; in leaf color they range from pale green to deep green to blue to deep mahogany red. Flower color also varies and can be white, yellow, rose, or red. The most well-known must be the cobweb houseleek, *Sempervivum arachnoideum*. It has a fine white webbing stretching from leaf tip to leaf tip; the individual rosettes are variable in size according to the form being grown but typically they are only 1 in. (2.5cm) in diameter. Some of the varieties have a very good coloring to their leaves, becoming quite reddened in the height of summer.

A rather choice sempervivum is *S. ciliosum* var. *borisii*. This is not very far off the previous species, *S. arachnoideum*, but it does have larger heads, up to 2¼ in. (6.5cm). This species does not like too much moisture during the winter months; it will become very gross, open and lax, if not kept dry. It does not require a heated greenhouse but will need protection from the winter moisture. Note: A clay pan is an essential for this plant.

There are about 30 species of sempervivum, but countless hybrids and cultivars. Some other genera tend to be lumped in with sempervivum by undiscerning people: Jovibarba, Rosularia, and Sempervivella.

Sempervirum ciliosum var. *borisii* **is a rather choice species which has recently become popular.**

Senecio
(Asteraceae)

These succulents are closely related to the groundsel weed. The inflorescences are composed of many small flowers which scarcely have petals, just stamens and anthers. They have the same seed-dispersal mechanism as groundsel: the tufts of silk with a seed attached at the send which is borne off by the wind to germinate a fair distance from its parent and so not pose a threat to the existence of the parent.

There are over 80 species of Senecio in cultivation. They come from central and southern Africa, Madagascar, the Canary Islands, Arabia, and Mexico to name the prime areas, although there are some species in other countries of the world.

Most of the species are easy to cultivate and are very often favored by beginners to the hobby. However as with other genera there are some from Madagascar that need extra warmth in winter.

The most commonly available species include *Senecio articulatus*, or candle plant. It is happy growing in almost any kind of condition, but too much food and water will result in the plants growing very tall or long, for this plant tends to clamber rather than keep upright. The new growth has lobed, glaucous leaves, which it sheds when resting. The flowers are cream colored and like many senecios, not very pleasant smelling. *S. rowleyanus*, or the string of beads plant, makes a good hanging-basket subject and will root from almost every leaf pair internode. It rarely flowers in captivity but it is not grown for the flower. *S. amaniensis* from Tanzania has large, round, flat leaves which are white. It can grow to a height of 24 in. (60cm); perhaps length would be a better description as this plant gets top heavy and is reluctant to stand up without support. The terminal inflorescence produced in late summer to autumn has orange flowers and smells atrocious. Cultivation is easy from shoots that appear in the leaf axils after the plant has flowered. Occasionally shoots appear from the base.

S. kleinia is a tree senecio from the Canary Islands, which can grow up to 10 ft. (3m). It grows during the autumn and winter, flowering at the beginning of its growing period.

Another tree senecio from Mexico is *S. praecox*. This has large palmate leaves and reaches a similar height to *S. kleinia*. The flowers on *S. praecox* are golden yellow. Whether they have an unpleasant smell or not we are unable to say. In cultivation this plant is prone to red spider mite and needs to be treated regularly and probably placed outdoors for the summer.

S. stapeliiformis is a very popular species, partly because it is easily propagated but also because it

has distinctive purple-red stripes up the stem. The flowers are a good strong scarlet color. *S.picticaulis* from Kenya, Tanzania, Sudan, and Ethiopia has a similar growth form to *S. articulatus*, perhaps not quite so jointed, but with cotton-candy pink flowers, and for that reason is worth including in your collection.

There are also senecios with underground tubers: *S. fulgens* and *S. nyikensis* are the two most common species. They have glaucous leaves, are evergreen, and have bright red flowers. Finally, we must mention a hairy-leaved or woolly leaved senecio, *S. haworthii*, also sometimes available under the name *Kleinia tomentosa*. In cultivation this plant should be

Senecio nyikensis is one of the more common species. They have impressive bright red flowers.

upright, but given the less than perfect light conditions that most of us have during the winter months, this plant tends to get rather lax. We have not seen this plant in flower in cultivation, but its flowers should be yellow.

Stomatium
(Aizoaceae)

Stomatiums come from South Africa, the Orange Free State, and Cape Province in particular. They are related to *Faucaria* but are generally smaller and have nocturnal flowers, whereas *Faucaria* are day flowering. These plants can be yellow or white flowered. Interestingly, the two flower color groups must attract different pollinators as their perfumes or aromas are quite different; the yellow flowers are quite citrusy, whereas the white flowers remind one of bananas.

They grow in the open, perhaps up against a rock, but they do get very baked. However, cultivation is easy. They are not at all finicky in their requirements, but a fairly well-drained compost is advisable, if they are not to become too lax. Each plant comprises a number of small rosettes of paired, alternate leaves. The leaf edges have white raised tubercles or warts and the white-flowered species tend to have a grayer appearance than the yellow flowered species, the leaves of which are a much brighter green.

Recommended yellow-flowering species are *Stomatium agninum* (no tubercles), *S. geoffreyi*, *S. integrum* (no tubercles), *S. jamesii*, *S. loganii*, and *S. pyrodorum* (supposedly smells of pears).

Recommended white-flowered species are *S. alboroseum*, *S. meyeri*, and *S. niveum*. Often these white flowers have a degree of pink in the petal tips, which is brought out by the cold as these plants usually flower in the late autumn, but may also flower in the early spring.

Cultivation is usually from seed, but cuttings may be taken.

Titanopsis

(Aizoaceae)

These little plants come from southern Namibia, west and central Cape Province. This small group of plants is highly adapted to its surroundings and conditions. Take note, they are not easy in captivity, requiring very well-drained compost with added limestone. More success may be had if the plants are grown in clay or terra cotta pots rather than plastic. That encourages the soil to dry out more quickly between waterings. Other points to remember are that maximum light conditions are needed for these little treasures, and do not overpot them.

The species available are *Titanopsis calcarea, T. fulleri, T. hugo-schlecteri*, T. *primosii*, and *T. schwantesii*. They have warty leaves to a lesser or greater extent. Sometimes this is on the edge of the leaf as in *T. fulleri*, sometimes randomly spaced on the face of the leaves. The plants are made up of several rosettes of alternating leaf pairs and branch in time. Leaf color is often bluish tinged with pink and the warts may be white. The roots are often thickened, hence better than average drainage is needed. The afternoon-opening flowers are mostly yellow, although *T. hugo-schlecteri* with leaves of almost a reddish-brown, has pinkish-orange flowers. *T. hugo-schlecteri* is also the most difficult species to

keep. The growing period is from August to December/January in the northern hemisphere, although if the atmosphere is very damp then it may be prudent to withhold watering until the humidity decreases.

Propagation is from seed, and the plants are unlikely to outgrow a 5 in. (12.5cm) pot.

Trichodiadema

(Aizoaceae)

The genus Trichodiadema is excellent for beginners; unfortunately there is a tendency for those who have been growing plants for some time to neglect or discard them. Why, we are not sure, perhaps because they have little rarity value. However, this group of some 30 species is from a fairly widespread area ranging from southern Namibia, western and southern Cape Province to one or two little pockets of plants in the Orange Free State in South Africa.

Characteristically these smallish plants have leaf tips that bear a cluster of dark brown, more or less spreading bristles, the diadem from which part of the plant name comes ("tricho" means hair).

The most rewarding species to grow must be *Trichodiadema bulbosum*. It has a tuberous rootstock that can be exposed above soil level in a pot or, better

Titanopsis calcarea is one of the readily available plants of this genus.

still, a bonsai container. If the top growth gets too lax or rampant the shears can be taken to it, but bear in mind that the purple flowers are borne on the new growth, so choose the time carefully to give the plant a trim.

T. densum is a plant that we acquired quite early in our collecting careers, and had to reacquire more recently. It makes a dense mound of short green leaves with the diadems at the leaf tips almost touching each other. This is a very good species for flowering.

T. stellatum is low growing and mat forming, having masses of pale purple flowers in late autumn. It almost looks dead when it is not growing, but a good soaking toward the end of summer will revitalize the plant in time for it to flower on time.

Not all trichodiademas have purple or pink flowers; some species, *T.mirabile* for one, have white flowers.

Propagation is from seed or cuttings, except for those that have annual growth.

There is an international specialty group which promotes the whole of the Aizoaceae and more information can be obtained joining them (see information sources on page 123).

Tylecodon

(Crassulaceae)

Until 1978 this genus of succulent plants was embraced in the genus *Cotyledon*. It does not take a crossword expert to realize that Tylecodon is an anagram of its former generic name. There was a reason why this group of plants was separated: cotyledons proper are not deciduous, rarely losing all their leaves according to the seasons, but retaining them to help the plants through hard times. Tylecodons on the other hand have caudices (treelike thickened stems), are deciduous and only come into growth when the conditions are right, i.e., when the rains come. They prefer to conserve their energies during drought by shedding their leaves and not losing moisture through them.

There are 30 species in this genus, and they come from the winter rainfall areas of southern Africa, Western Cape Province and Namibia. These plants grow and flower in the winter months in the UK, and therefore need a minimum temperature of 41°F (5°C). They like a fairly well-drained soil mixture, although they are not too fussy.

Some of the species are quite tiny: *Tylecodon schaeferianus* reaches only 6 in. (15cm) in height. Others, such as *T. paniculatus*, can reach a height of 5 ft. (1.5m) in the wild. So, it is important to select the species to suit your conditions.

The smaller-growing species include *T. bucholzianus*, very slow growing, clumping readily and resembling a small group of brown corals when resting and without leaves; *T. schaeferianus*, also rejoicing in the name of *T. sinus-alexandri*, with white or pink flowers, and small, roundish leaves, rather loosely attached.

The larger-growing species include: *T. cacalioides*, a tree reaching one meter; *T. paniculatus*, a tree to 5 ft. (1.5m) high and 23½ in. (60cm) in diameter; *T. reticulatus*, a tree growing to 5¾ ft. (1.75m) high, looking as though it is festooned on top with barbed wire when it flowers; and *T. wallichii*, treelike, attaining 3¼ ft. (1m) in height.

Yucca
(Agavaceae)

Yuccas, like agaves, come from the Americas. They can be relatively small, *Yucca endlichiana* having leaves which come from ground level and are about 12 in. (30cm) tall, to the giant *Y. brevifolia* (the joshua tree), which attains a height of 25 ft. (7.5m) with age and can be quite a size across having many heads. Neither of these species will do well in a wet climate.

The most common species must be *Y. elata*, very frequently sold as a houseplant. It is also sold as a small section of stem or a little "log" which is sealed with wax at both ends to conserve moisture. Rarely does this piece of wood fail to root, so tenacious is it in its desire to live. As a houseplant it will

Yucca filamentosa, in its variegated form, is one of the more commonly found garden species.

soon outgrow its welcome and become an embarrassment. With age the plant base thickens considerably and gets to the point where it is difficult to find a pot in which to plant it. It will also, if kept long enough, get too tall for the average-height room. We suspect that eventually such plants are left outside for the winter and so die.

The species most often seen in garden centers and hence gardens, are *Y. gloriosa, Y. flaccida,* and *Y. filamentosa*. The first two species are the larger growing and will make large clumps or bushes, multiplying up after flowering. *Y. gloriosa* will also sucker from underground. They do not seem to be fussy about what soil type they grow in, but we have known *Y. gloriosa* to rot off at the base if kept too wet: make sure that leaf debris is kept away from the base to avoid this. *Y. filamentosa* is available as a plain green-leaved variety or more interestingly a variegated form, such as "ivory."

In the greenhouse the following species can be accommodated: *Y. glauca, Y. endlichiana, Y. carnerosana, Y. whipplei, Y. harrimaniae,* and *Y. baccata.*

Y. glauca and *Y. whipplei* should be hardy; if these are grown from seed it would be worthwhile experimenting with the odd seedling to test its hardiness. All benefit from being outdoors for the summer.

All of these plants will flower, perhaps not every year but most years. The flowers are usually a creamy white with occasionally hints of pink. The flowers are borne on a tall stem and are roughly bell-shaped and usually hang down, although in some species the flower are upright against the stem. The flowers are rich in nectar and, when grown in the open, may attract aphids, which in turn attract ants.

A word of caution about the leaves on these plants: in the species which have rigid leaves there is usually a very sharp tip on the end. So wherever they are grown, keep these plants toward the back of the border or staging.

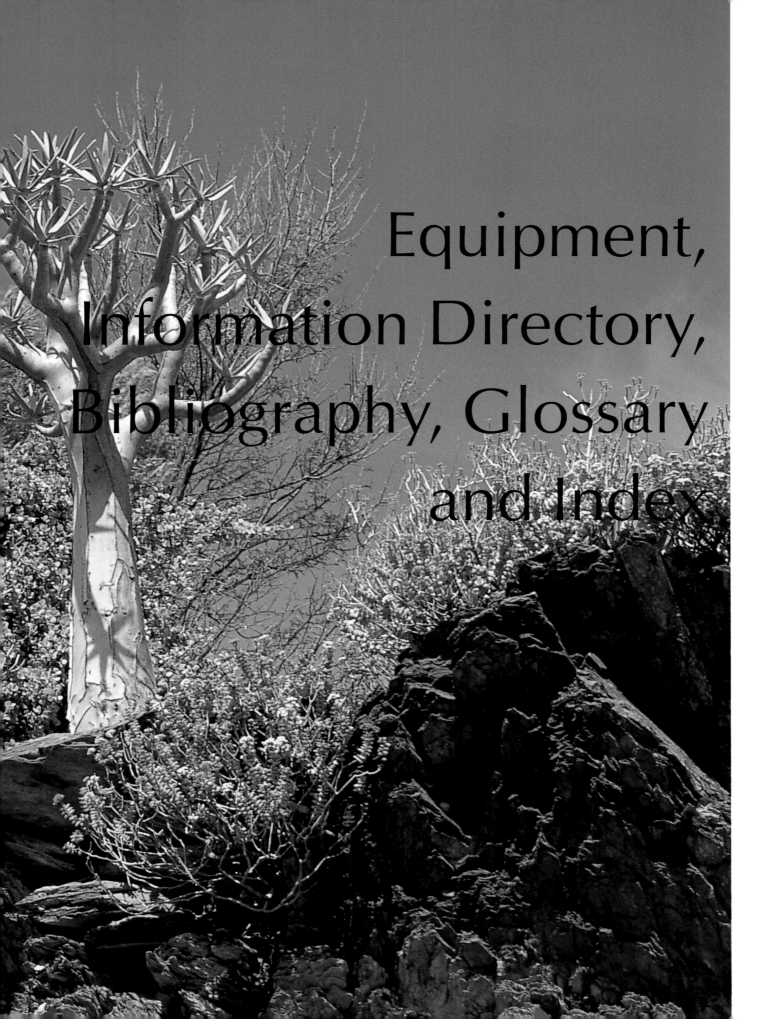

Equipment,
Information Directory,
Bibliography, Glossary
and Index

1. Pair of regular pruning shears for taking larger cuttings.

2. Dibble for planting small seedlings or cuttings.

3. Plastic scoop for putting soil around a plant or for top dressing with small gravel.

4. Large tweezers for grabbing very spiny plants.

5. Folding pruning saw for large, woody cuttings.

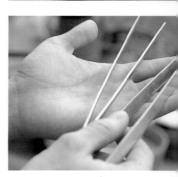

Equipment

Above: A pair of grapevine shears with very fine blades, ideal for taking small cuttings.

Having the right tools at hand will always make the task of looking after your cacti and succulents much easier.

Thermometer. For a greenhouse, conservatory, or simply a window sill collection

Watering can. A can with a long spout with a fine rose would be a boon. A smaller version will help you to deliver the correct amount of water to a plant.

Mister. Small handheld mister will be useful for spraying insecticides and zapping pests. They are also useful for adding moisture to the atmosphere on dry, hot days.

Plastic tub. Invest in a large one to mix your compost in or to empty out ready-to-use blends that you have purchased.

Tweezers. Grasping hold of pots can be tricky, particularly if the spines are so long that they extend over the rim. A pair of heavy-duty tweezers or grabbers will be useful not only for handling pots but also for handling cuttings of taller plants. Smaller tweezers are good for pulling spines out of hands, etc.

Knives. A selection of sharp, clean knives for taking cuttings is useful.

Labels and pens. Make sure your plants are labeled with a lightproof

and waterproof pen and record as much data as possible.

Supports. For clambering plants, trellis supports are needed along with plastic-covered ties.

Stakes. With really large plants some form of support may be necessary, particularly if they are being moved around. Some of the cacti do not have much of a woody core and easily snap off.

Information Directory

BOOKS
To find more information on cacti and succulents, there is a fairly extensive bibliography on page 124. Some of these books are published in small numbers by relatively obscure publishers. If you cannot obtain them through your local book dealers try the following contacts:

USA: Rainbow Gardens Bookshop,
444 E. Taylor St., Vista,
CA 92084.
Tel: (760) 758-4290; *fax:* (760) 945-8934; *email:* rbgdns@aol.com

UK: Whitestone Gardens,
The Cactus Houses,
Sutton-Under-Whitestonecliffe,
Thirsk, N. Yorks, YO7 2PZ.
Tel: (+44) 1845 597467; *fax:* (+44) 1845 597035;
email: roy@whitestn.demon.co.uk

Germany: Versngeschaft fur Botanische Fachliteratur,
Lockfinke 7,
D-42111 Wuppertal,
Germany

SOCIETIES
Prime sources of information are the regular journals published by cactus and succulent societies in various countries. The principal ones are listed below:

The Cactus and Succulent Society of America,
566 Gepke Parkway,
Des Moines, IA 50320-6818,
U.S.A.
Tel: (515) 285-6818;
fax: (515) 285-7760;
e-mail: mpfusaro@aol.com
Bimonthly journal of approximately 40 pages; many affiliated clubs in the U.S.A. and Canada.

The British Cactus and Succulent Society,
15 Brentwood Crescent,
Hull Road,
York, YO1 5HU, U.K.
Tel: (+44) 1904 410512;
fax: (+44) 1444 454061
email: bcss@mace.demon.co.uk
Quarterly journal of approximately 50 pages—branches throughout the UK and Republic of Ireland.

The Cactus and Succulent Society of New Zealand,
20A Tawera Road,
Greenlane,
Auckland,
New Zealand
Tel: (09) 520 3442
Quarterly journal; several branches in New Zealand.

The Succulent Society of South Africa,
Private Bag X10,
0011 Brooklyn,
South Africa.
Tel & fax: (012) 98 3588;
email: kambroo@cis.co.za
Quarterly journal.

Assocociazone Italiana Amatori delle Piante Succelente (AIAS),
Via S.Pietro 5,
I-00185 Roma,
Italy.
Tel: 06-49913326.
Quarterly journal, 35-40 pages, in Italian; a number of regional groups.

Kakteen und andere Sukkulenten,
Geshaftsstele,
Betenriedweg 44, D-72800,
Eningen unter Achalm,
Germany.
Tel: 0 71 21 88 05 10.
Joint monthly journal of the German, Swiss and Austrian cactus societies, in German. Approximately 25 pages. The societies have many groups in Germany, Austria and Switzerland.

Succulenta,
Prins Willem-Alexanderlaan 104, 6721 AE Bennekom,
Holland.
Quarterly journal, in Dutch. Approximately 35 pages. Many local groups in Holland.

THE INTERNET
A good source of up to date information is available on the Internet. The authors of this book maintain a website called the Cactus and Succulent Plant Mall which contains links to most of the cactus and succulent information available electronically. This is in English, French, German, Italian, Spanish, Dutch and Japanese. It can be reached at:
http://www.cactus-mall.com

There is also an excellent electronic mailing list on cacti and succulents which is freely available to anyone with email access. It can be joined by sending the message:
subscribe cacti_etc [your name]
to: listserv@opus.hpl.hp.com.

SPECIAL-INTEREST GROUPS
Devotees of certain popular group of succulent plants have formed international societies which specialise in their interests. The following groups publish periodic journals:

The Mammillaria Society,
28 Winfield Grove,
Newdigate,
Surrey,
England RH5 5AZ.
email: 106520.1004@compuserve.com
The International Asclepiad Society,
2 Keymer Court,
Burgess Hill,
West Sussex,
England RH15 0AA.
email: ias@mace.demon.co.uk
Covers all Asclepiadaceae.

The Haworthia Society,
15 Cattistock Close,
Guisborough,
Cleveland,
England TS14 7NL.
email: HMays@onyxnet.co.uk
Covers Aloes in addition to Bulbines, Haworthias and Gasterias.

The Chileans,
32 Forest Lane,
Kirklevington,
Yarm, England TS15 9LY
Covers all South American cacti.

The Mesemb Study Group,
Brenfield,
Bolney Road,
Ansty,
West Sussex,
England RH17 5AW.
email: msg@mace.demon.co.uk
Covers all Mesembryanthemaceae.

The Euphorbiaceae Study Group,
11 Shaftesbury Avenue,
Penketh,
Warrington,
Cheshire,
England WA5 2PD.
email: 011723.3005@compuserve.com

COMMERCIAL INTEREST
Interest in the commercial cultivation of cacti in arid areas is on the increase. A number of different cactus fruits are cultivated for direct consumption and for turning into products such as jam, candy or drinks.

The pads of opuntias are used as a vegetable and also as cattle fodder. Succulent plants have also been exploited as sources for fibre (agaves), alcoholic drinks (tequila) and pharmaceutical and cosmetic products (eg. Aloe vera).

The organisation studying these aspects is:

The Professional Association for Cactus Development (PACD),
PO Box 461045, San Antonio,
TX 78246-1045,
USA

Bibliography

The following is a list of the cactus and succulent literature which we consult most frequently. This is by no means exhaustive as it does not contain many Floras which have been published on particular areas where succulent plants are found:

Anderson, E. F., Montes, S.A., Taylor, N.P., *Threatened Cacti of Mexico*, Royal Botanic Gardens Kew, 1994
ISBN 0 947643 69 9

Anderson, E. F., *Peyote: The Divine Cactus*, University of Arizona Press
ISBN 0 8165 1653 7

Backeberg, C., *Cactus Lexicon*, Blandford Press, 1966
ISBN 0 7137 0840 9

Bally, P. R. O., *The Genus Monadenium*, Benteli Publishers, Berne, 1961

Bayer, M. B., *The New Haworthia Handbook*, National Botanic Gardens of South Africa, 1982
ISBN 0 620 05632 0

Benson, L., *The Cacti of the United States and Canada*, Stanford University Press, 1982
ISBN 0 8047 0863 0

Borg, J., *Cacti*, Blandford Press, Third Edition, 1959.
Bregman, R., *The Genus Matucana*, A.A. Balkema, 1996
ISBN 90 5410 638 7

Britton, N. L. and Rose, J. N. *The Cactaceae*, The Carnegie Institute of Washington, 1919

Buining, A. F. H., *Discocactus, Succulenta*

Buxbaum, F., *Cactus Culture Based on Biology*, Blandford Press, 1958

Buxbaum, F., *Morphology of Cacti*, Abbey Garden Press, 1959

Cole, D.T., *Lithops: Flowering Stones*, Russel Friedman Books, 1988 ISBN 0 620 09678 0

Cullmann, W., Götz, E., and Gröner, G., *The Encyclopedia of Cacti*, Alphabooks, 1984
ISBN 0 906670 37 3

Dyer, R. A., *Ceropegia, Brachystelma and Riocreuxia in Southern Africa*, A. A. Balkema, 1983
ISBN 90 6191 227 X

Eggli, U., *Glossary of Botanical Terms with special reference to Succulent Plants*, The British Cactus and Succulent Society, 1993
ISBN 0 902099 22 1

Eggli, U., *Sukkulenten*, Eugen Ulmer, 1994
ISBN 3 8001 6512 0

Gentry, H. S., *Agaves of Continental North America*, University of Arizona Press, 1982
ISBN 0 8165 0775 9

Hammer, S.A., *The Genus Conophytum: A Conograph*, Succulent Plant Publications Pretoria, 1993
ISBN 0 620 17634 2

Hewitt, T., *The Complete Book of Cacti & Succulents*, Dorling Kindersley, 1993
ISBN 0 7513 0049 7

Higgins, V., *Crassulas in Cultivation*, Blandford Press, 1964

Hodoba, T. B., *Growing Desert Plants: from Windowsill to Garden*, Red Crane Books, 1995
ISBN 1 878610 54 6

Jacobsen, H., *A Handbook of Succulent Plants*, Blandford Press, 1960.

Jacobsen, H., *Lexicon of Succulent Plants*, Blandford Press Ltd., 1974
ISBN 07137 0652 X

Lawrie, I., *Coryphantha and Associated Genera*, The Mammillaria Society, 1988

Mace, T., *Notocactus*, National Cactus and Succulent Society, Sussex Zone, 1975

MacMillan, A. J. S., and Horobin, J. F., *Christmas Cacti: The genus Schlumbergera and its hybrids*, 1995, David Hunt ISBN 0 9517234 6 4

Nel, G. C., *The Gibbaeum Handbook*, Blandford Press, 1953

Nobel, P. S., *The Environmental Biology of Agaves and Cacti*, Cambridge University Press, 1988
ISBN 0 521 34322 4

Pilbeam, J., *Mammillaria: A Collectors' Guide*, B. T. Batsford Ltd, 1981
ISBN 0 7134 3987 5

Pilbeam, J., *Sulcorebutia and Weingartia: A Collectors' Guide*, B.T. Batsford Ltd, 1985
ISBN 0 7134 4672 2

Pilbeam, J., *Thelocactus*, Cirio Publishing Services Ltd., 1996
ISBN 0 9528302 0 5

Rauh, W., *Succulent and Xerophytic Plants of Madagascar* (Vol1), Strawberry Press, 1995
ISBN 0 912647 14 0

Rausch, W., *Lobivia*, W Rausch, 1975

Rowley, G. D., *Anacampseros, Avonia, Grahamia*, The British Cactus and Succulent Society, 1995
ISBN 0 902099 29 9

Rowley, G. D., *A History of Succulent Plants*, Strawberry Press, 1997
ISBN 0 912647 16 0

Rowley, G. D., *Caudiciform and Pachycaul Succulents*, Strawberry Press, 1987 ISBN 0 912647 03 5

Rowley, G. D., *Didiereaceae: 'Cacti of the Old World'*, The British Cactus and Succulent Society, 1992
ISBN 0 902099 20 5

Rowley, G. D., *Name that Succulent*, Stanley Thornes (Publishers) Ltd., 1980 ISBN 0 85950 447 6

Rowley, G. D., *Succulent Compositae*, Strawberry Press, 1994
ISBN 0 912647 12 4

Rowley, G. D., *The Adenium and Pachypodium Handbook*, The British Cactus and Succulent Society, 1983
ISBN 0 902099 07 8

Reynolds, G. W., *The Aloes of South Africa*, A. A. Balkema, 1974
ISBN 0 86961 064 3

Reynolds, G. W., *The Aloes of Tropical Africa and Madagascar*, The Aloes Book Fund, 1966

Schwantes, G., *The Cultivation of the Mesembryanthemaceae*, Blandford Press, 1954

Schulz, R. and Kapitany, A., *Copiapoa in their Environment*, Published by the authors, 1996

Schwartz *et al.*, H., *The Euphorbia Journal*, Vols 1-10, Strawberry Press, 1983-1997

Spain, J., *Growing Winter Hardy Cacti*, 1994

Stephenson, R., *Sedum: Cultivated Stonecrops*, Timber Press Inc., 1994 ISBN 0 88192 238 2

Storms, E., *The New Growing the Mesembs*, Ed Storms Inc., 1986

van Jaarsveld, E., *Gasterias of Southern Africa*, Fernwood Press, 1994 ISBN 1 874950 01 6

Walther, E., *Echeveria*, California Academy of Sciences, 1972

White A., and Sloane, B. L., *The Stapelieae*, Abbey San Encino Press, 1937

Zappi, D. C., *Pilosocereus (Cactaceae): The Genus in Brazil*, 1994, David Hunt ISBN 0 9517234 4 8

Glossary

Adventitious
An organ occurring in an unusual place, e.g., adventitious bud or plantlets—*Bryophyllum tubiflorum*; adventitious roots.

Areole
The cushion of spines, almost always with fine hairs, which is characteristic of cacti. They represent short modified shoots.

Axil
The angle between the stem and a leaf, also the region at the base of and between the tubercles. Hairs, bristles, side shoots or flowers may be produced at the axils.

Bract
Modified leaf at the base of a flower.

Cactophile
Person who likes cacti.

Caudex
Massively enlarged portion of stems and sometimes roots often of a succulent nature.

Cephalium
A distinctly separate region of certain cactus species, usually with densely bristly or woolly areoles, from which the flowers are produced.

Chlorosis
A more or less distinct lack of chlorophyll leading to the plant having a sickly yellow color. Often a symptom of deficiency of a micro-nutrient such as iron or boron.

Cristate
Having abnormal fasciated or fanlike growth due to an elongated instead of pointlike growing point.

Deltoid
Shaped like the Greek letter D (Delta).

Dichotomous
With two equal or similar choices, branched in two with two equal branches, forked.

Ephemeral
Short lived

Epicuticular
"On the ... cuticle," especially epicuticular wax = a layer of wax (continuous, powdery [farinose], or variously structured into plates, coils, etc.) covering the ... cuticle on the outer surface.

Epiphytic
Growing on other plants, but not parasitic on them.

Etiolated
A type of abnormally elongated growth, paler green due to a partial lack of chlorophyll because of insufficient light.

Excrescence
Outgrowth, warty appendage, protuberance.

Farina
A flourlike, mealy white powder

Fasciated
Having abnormal growth with flattened and laterally expanded stems, or irregular stems; caused by abnormal divisions of the growing point.

Fissure
The aperture between two otherwise united leaves.

Glaucous
Covered with a grayish white or bluish white/green bloom

Glochids
Very fine spines covered with microscopically small barbs, and typical of the Opuntioideae sub-family.

Glutinous
Sticky, gluelike

Hygrochastic
Moving of plant parts caused by absorbing water or drying out.

Inflorescence
A plant branch that carries the flowers.

Keeled
Having a raised ridge, like the keel of a ship.

Lanceolate
Shaped like a lance.

Monocarpic
Flowering once at the end of a life span and then dying after the fruits have ripened.

Ovary
The bottom part of the cactus flower with an internal cavity containing the ovules.

Peduncle
The main stalk of a whole inflorescence.

Photosynthesis
A physiological process carried out by green plants in which solar energy is used to convert carbon dioxide and water into sugars (food) with the help of chlorophyll.

Pruinose
Covered with a fine whitish slightly powdery layer like a plum (due to a fine layer of epicuticular wax).

Pubescent
Having short hairs or down.

Ribs
Parts of the body of a cactus forming raised ridges running more or less vertically.

Scales
External structures, often formed on the ovary and the tube of cactus flowers.

Scion
The upper part of a graft, i.e., the piece grafted onto a more robust grafting stock.

Serrated
With sawlike teeth.

Spathulate
Spatula shaped, i.e.. tapering from a rounded apex into a gradually narrowing stalk.

Spines
In the botanical sense superficial growths on the stems or leaves, as opposed to thorns, which are modified leaves or stems. The spines of cacti should really be termed thorns, as they are modified leaves.

Succulent
Thick-fleshed and capable of storing large quantities of water.

Tube
The humps, or warts, which occur on the stems of many cacti and which bear areoles. In some cacti such as *Mammillaria*, the tubercles are the remains of ribs that have become deeply notched.

Tubercles
An underground fleshy stem or stem segment with several buds, e.g., a potato; or a fleshy root or root part.

Vascular bundle
A bundle of tissue consisting of elongated cells which serve to transport water and food. In succulent dicotyledons these can be seen as an annular arrangement of fine threads in the cross section of the stem.

Viscid
Sticky, glutinous

Xerophyte
Any plant showing some degree of adaption to environments with very little precipitation.

Zygomorphic flowers
Bilaterally symmetrical flowers as opposed to flowers with full circular symmetry.

Index

CACTUS AND SUCCULENTS

ACKNOWLEDGMENTS

Artwork by Fiona Fraser

PHOTOGRAPHIC ACKNOWLEDGMENTS
AKG, London: 23
Anthony Blake Photo Library/Peter Cassidy: 25 Bottom
Corbis UK Ltd/Gianni Dagli Orti: 20
E.T. Archive: 24, 25 Top
Tony Mace: 9, 15 Bottom, 16 Bottom, 26-27, 43, 56, 66, 71
Reed Consumer Books Ltd.: 2-3, 6-7, 17, 67 Top, 67
Bottom, 72 Bottom, 72 Top, 73 Top, 77 Bottom, 77 Top, 78
Top, 79 Top, 81 Top, 86 Top, 87 Bottom, 88, 89 Bottom, 90
Top, 119, 120-121
Peter Myers: Cover, Front Endpaper, Back Endpaper, 1, 4-5,
8-9, 10-11, 15 Top, 16 Top, 18, 19, 29, 30, 31, 33, 34
Bottom, 34 Top, 35 Bottom, 35 Center, 35 Top, 36, 39, 40-
41, 42, 44 Top, 44 Bottom, 46-47, 49, 50, 51, 52, 54-55, 57,
58-59, 60-61, 61, 62 Bottom, 62 Top, 63, 64, 65, 68, 69, 70
Bottom, 70 Top, 73 Bottom, 75, 76, 78 Bottom, 79 Bottom,
80, 81 Bottom, 82, 83, 84, 85, 86 Bottom, 87 Top, 89 Top
Left, 89 Top Right, 90 Bottom, 91, 92 Center, 92 Top, 92
Bottom, 93, 94, 95, 96, 97, 98, 99, 100, 101, 103, 104
Bottom, 104 Top, 105, 106 Top, 106 Bottom, 107, 108, 109,
110, 111, 112, 113, 115, 116, 117, 118, 122 Center Right, 122
Top Left, 122 Top Right, 122 Top Center Right, 122 Bottom
Right, 122 Bottom Center Right
N.J. Saunders: 22